REMEMBERING

Our Shared Legacy from the First World War

Edited by Eamonn Baker

This book has received financial support from the Northern Ireland Community Relations Council which aims to promote a pluralist society characterised by equity, respect for diversity and interdependence. The views expressed do not necessarily reflect those of the Council.

This publication has been supported financially by Derry City Council through its Heritage and Museum Service. The views expressed do not necessarily reflect those of the Council.

First Published in 2009
by YES! Publications
www.yespublications.org
10-12 Bishop Street
Derry/Londonderry BT48 6PW
Tel: 028 71261941
www.yespublications.org

Cover photograph : Courtesy of John McDaid (stillphotos.co.uk)
Back cover image : Courtesy of Marion Ross

ISBN: 978-1-873832-40-0

Community Relations Council

CONTENTS

INTRODUCTION

Remembering has grown out of the innovative and extensive research into the local impact of the First World War conducted over the past few years by Trevor Temple, staff member of the North West War Memorial Project. This community-based project was developed by Holywell Trust and funded by the Heritage Lottery Fund.

Remembering recalls the lives and times of young local men (and sometimes not so young men), from both major community traditions here who volunteered for service in the British Army during the First World War, many of whom fought and died in France, Belgium, Gallipoli and elsewhere. Each of these men had his own motivation for enlisting – "Ulster" patriotism, fighting for King and Country, support for Carson and resistance to the Home Rule; "Irish" patriotism, support for Redmond, fighting for "the freedom of small nations" and Irish independence; poverty no doubt motivated many; ties of friendship many more. Confronted by the unrelenting day to day horrors of trench warfare, incessant shelling, lethal gas, unimaginable casualty levels, survival, leavened by a fierce spirit of altruism, may finally have become the dominant motivation. As many as 5000 men, out of a total population then of around 40,000, left Derry/Londonderry to serve in the First World War. Over 1000 of these were killed - 2.5 % of the city's population. This mountainous death toll traumatised our city long before trauma counselling was even heard of. The bereaved from both traditions relied heavily upon their families and their churches for support and care. Many of those who returned were recovering from wounds, were amputees or shell-shocked, were disturbed and silent. Heroic self-sacrifice, particularly at the Somme, was swiftly acknowledged within the Unionist tradition. As first, the War of Independence, then partition and civil war convulsed Ireland, some First World War veterans from the Nationalist tradition embroiled themselves in these struggles whilst others returned to suspicion, or perhaps worse, indifference within their own community. Ironically, some survivors of the First World War were to meet their deaths on the streets of their own city during the bloody riots of 1920.

Remembering consists of edited interviews with members of twenty local families who lost loved ones to the First World War. Without their generous commitment and openness, this book would not have been possible. Each interviewee has shared intimate family details which previously had remained hidden from our collective view. Many interviewees had researched the life and times of their predecessor enabling readers of *Remembering* to gather a more rounded human picture both of those who went off to war and of those who were left behind. We learn for example of Wesley Maultsaid's footballing skills, of Holmes Haslett's athletic prowess, racing down the Culmore Road ahead of the mail boat on the waters of the Foyle, of Denis Doherty's working life at McCullagh's in Waterloo Place, and on the docks, of George Hasson "sweeping" around the city. We are privileged to gain access to the private family photographs, documents, keep-sakes, memorabilia used to illustrate this publication.

Though all of the interviews were conducted in the spring of 2009, more than ninety years after Armistice Day 1918, it quickly became clear that many of the interviewees were grieving over the loss of their grandfather, grand-uncle, uncle (whom they, of course, had never known personally) in ways which suggested that the family loss had never been fully resolved. Roy Arbuckle speaks eloquently here of the tears that sprang to the eyes of audience members when handed poppies by khaki-clad actors during the opening scene of the community play, "Home for Christmas" and asked to "*Remember.*"

Our publication also invites remembrance and acknowledgement both of those men from our community, from Derry and from Londonderry, who served and those who died during the First World War. We also remember and acknowledge their families who became the guardians of the family narratives shared here.

ACKNOWLEDGEMENTS

Trevor Temple has been involved in almost every interview providing constant support and insight.

Mary McElhinney, staff member of the North West War Memorial Project also played a key role within the interview process.

Bridget O'Toole Walsh kindly interviewed Frank McGuinness, author of "Observe the Sons of Ulster Marching Towards the Somme".

The kind permission of Tracey McRory, Richard Laird and the estate of the late Sam Starrett, to reproduce words and music of the songs: "John Condon" and "From the Somme back to the Foyle". Copyright Songshed.

Our thanks to Maura Craig and Patricia McAdams of the Central Library for their help and support in accessing the Bigger McDonald Collection.

The North West War Memorial Project also gratefully acknowledges the support of award-winning film-maker, Alessandro Negrini, the sterling work of Jennifer McClarey who transcribed all of the audio-tapes, the photography of Jackie McColgan, Yes! Publications and the ongoing support of Fionnuala Deane of Yes! Publications and of Eamonn Deane, Holywell Trust director who, "back in the day" envisioned this publication.

The creative skills, commitment and energy of graphic designer, Eugene Duffy, were vital to the completion of *Remembering*.

Finally the editor wishes to express his gratitude to the management committee of Community Development Learning Initiative for their support in the development and preparation of this publication.

TO THE MEMBERS

OF THE

ULSTER VOLUNTEER FORCE

I greatly appreciate the action of our Volunteers in rallying so enthusiastically to my call for Defenders of the Empire. To those who have not already responded to that call and are eligible and can go, I say—QUIT YOURSELVES LIKE MEN AND COMPLY WITH YOUR COUNTRY'S DEMAND.

Enlist at once for the Ulster Division in Lord Kitchener's Army for the period of the War.

You were formed to defend our citizenship in the United Kingdom and the Empire, and so preserve our civil and religious liberty. Now the United Kingdom and the Empire are threatened we must fight with our fellow-Britishers until victory is assured.

To those Loyalists who are not eligible or cannot go I appeal that they shall fill up the vacancies in the U.V.F. ranks caused by those going to the Front, so that we may maintain in fullest efficiency the Ulster Volunteer Force to protect your homes and hearths—that is a duty we owe to the Volunteers who go abroad to fight the country's battles. Let every Loyalist be faithful to the trust, and by each one doing his duty our country will be saved and our own interests preserved.

NO SURRENDER.

GOD SAVE THE KING.

EDWARD CARSON.

Old Town Hall, Belfast,
7th September, 1914.

Edward Carson's rallying call to all members of the UVF to "enlist at once" in the Ulster Division for the "period of the war".

Billy Sinclair remembers

Andrew, Hugh, Thomas and John Sinclair

Andrew, Hugh, Thomas and John Sinclair from Hawthorn Terrace. Five brothers served during the First World War and these four lost their lives. Because of this tragedy, the fifth brother, Dick (Billy's father), was brought back to England and did home service for the last couple of months of the war.

❝ My father, Dick Sinclair, lost four of his brothers, Andrew, Hugh, Thomas and John during the First World War. The only good thing, if you understand what I mean, was that my granny Sinclair had died before any of the boys were killed so she didn't have to suffer that terrible loss. My grandfather Archie, already widowed, must have had a shocking time. He died in 1924, maybe from a broken heart.

Here is a letter from my Uncle Andy to my mother, dated 2nd September 1918.

Dear sister,

Just received your very welcome letter dated 25 August and was glad to see by it that you are all well at home as this leaves me in the pink and enjoying life as much as possible under the circumstances. I'm very happy because after all we are going to win the war and I don't think it will take us much longer. Well Mary Anne, I feel quite sorry for you, and I say it is a shame sending Dick

France
Sept. 2nd 1918.

Dear sister

Just received of your very welcome
letter dated 26th Aug and was glad to see
by it that you were all well at home
as this leaves me in the pink, and
enjoying life as well as possible under
the circumstances and fairly happy because
I think oft and all we are going to win
the war, and I dont think it will take
us much longer. Well sister dear dont
you worry for you and Joey it wont be a thing
resting. Vicious again as it is so little to
thing will do for us now, as to be one of us
at the east home, after all we have suffered
but I think the army is like most of the
people these times, the must one care for
them the more they care you to do

but you can too too my word for it, that in
future I am going to do our little as possible for
them, but dear sister dont you worry that much
for I am sure Dick will be able to take care of
himself all right as I very sure one would
often as sure to the front for their last I
do not wish never to his own father asks
me to have been a little and I will not let him go
and tell him I am waiting for a letter with his
own address. Well you I am willing him
this year all like Dick, and in no case is hard
after this if you will get the big order

Well sister this is my my own dear
the way we turn little and my dear all
will some day to hear from you again soon
with best love to the children and you, and
all us here,
          I Remain
               Your loving brother
                    Andy.
               XXX XXXXX

Letter from Andy Sinclair to his sister-in-law Mary-Anne, dated September 2nd, 1918. Andy was killed less than two weeks after he had written this letter.

out again as it is as little as they could do as to let one of us stop at home, after all we have suffered. But I think the army is like most of the people these times, the more one does for them the more they ask you. But you can take my word for it, in future I am going to do as little as possible for them. Dear sister, don't worry too much, for I'm sure Dick will be able to take care of himself so be easy in your mind. When you are writing to him Mary Anne tell him I could not write in answer to his last letter as he might have been shifted and would not have got it. And tell him I am waiting for a letter with his new address. Well now Mary Anne, I know that you all like May and as soon as I can after the war, you will get a big night. Well now, there's nothing more I have to say so hoping this will find you all well, I'm hoping to hear from you again soon, with best love to the children, and you, and all at home, your loving brother, Andy. XXXXXXXXX

Andy addresses my mother as 'my sister Mary Anne'. She was, in fact, his sister-in-law but he always refers to her as 'my sister'. They must have been very close. Less than two weeks later, on September 13th, Andy himself was killed in action, the fourth brother to die. My grandfather then applied to the War Office and my father was brought home from the front to the south of England where he spent the last few weeks of the war.

My grandfather, Archie Sinclair, was a tinsmith who, having worked in the shipyard in Glasgow, came here about 1880 I think and worked in Brewster's Bakery, making biscuit tins. Andy was born in Derry. The rest of the family were born in Glasgow. Tommy and Hugh had emigrated to Canada when they were very young, one of them was only fifteen. Then in 1914 they joined up to one of the Scottish regiments, the Canadian Highlanders.

I was born in 1922. I never really knew anything about my uncles. All I knew was that my father had lost four brothers in the First World War. I knew this growing up but I didn't know how they died, or where they died, until my own brother Archie's death in February 1998, eighty years after the war. We were all reared up on Hawthorn Terrace and he then lived in a bungalow in Glenbank Road, where he died.

Archie always kept a wooden box. I knew it was there but I didn't know what was in it. Archie had everything my mother had collected, all the bits and pieces from my uncles - wee personal things, death certificates, photographs, letters, postcards from the front. I took the photographs to a neighbour, Nan Burney, who knew my four uncles. Nan lived in Glasgow Terrace and she was able to identify them all from the photographs.

My father never talked about losing his brothers. Can you imagine losing four brothers? And Andy says in his letter *'in future I am going to do as little as possible for them'*. He was hurting too.

There were nine of us. What you would have called an average family! We lost my sister Evelyn. She died in 1924, from pleurisy. I wasn't the youngest. I have a brother Andrew twelve years younger than me. I'm eighty-six, he's seventy-four. He lives in Peterborough now. My mother gave him the brothers' medals but he wasn't interested in them. When I was over in Peterborough on holiday, I was in his workshop out the back, opened an old tin and there were all the medals, packed in.

They were in a terrible state. I brought them home and they've been cared for since, well cared for.

Of the four brothers who were killed, Johnny was the only one already married. He married Becky Hamilton. They had no family, and Johnny's medals are the only ones I'm missing. Becky lived for a long time after. She never married again and they had no family. I'm very grieved because I can't get those medals to complete the set. I would get them mounted but I wouldn't mount them unless I had the whole five of them. I want all the medals to complete the set and then have them mounted. I might even give them over to the Inniskillings.

Claremont Presbyterian Church has been closed now for many years. Upstairs in the church there was a big brass plaque with the names of members of that congregation who had died in the First World War inscribed upon it. My uncles' names are on it, Andrew, Hugh, John and Tommy Sinclair. That plaque from Claremont Church is now installed in First Derry Presbyterian Church. Reverend David Latimer is responsible for that I imagine. I am not a member of that church though. I'm Church of Ireland. I attended Christ Church School from when I was four. So did all my family, brothers and sisters, sons and daughters. My granny and granda Kyle were married in Christ Church and my father and mother were married in Christ Church, though me and Rita met and married in England in 1943 during the war. Rita brought me home to Derry because she got scared with the doodlebug bombs raining down. She brought me home to "my ma". In 1939 I had wanted to join the army. I was seventeen. My father said to me "*I lost four brothers in the last war. I don't want to lose you in this one.*" He said this in Hawthorn Terrace. He was letting me know that our family had done their part. That was one of the few times he mentioned his brothers. In those days your father was "the law." You answered to your father and mother. I did the next best thing. I worked for the war effort for four years in England until I met Rita.

I'm a good loyal Prod but I have a cousin who was killed on Bloody Sunday - John Young. His grandfather and my granny were brother and sister. I was never in the Orange Order or Apprentice Boys nor anything like that. We are church going. I go to Christ Church. I love singing in church and I love taking part in the service but my eyesight is going that bad I have a large print hymn book and prayer book. One Sunday I couldn't see, I just filled up and I haven't gone back to church on a Sunday since. I go on Thursday morning for Communion at half past ten.

In the photograph on the right, you see my father and mother pictured at Bundoran fifty odd years ago. They were a handsome couple. My father passed on in 1969. He was eighty-one years old and still living in Hawthorn Terrace. My mother died in 1979, she was eighty-nine. She was a great person. She never went to church but she was a fantastic Christian. She loved giving. My father worked six nights a week always in Hunter's. He was the ovens man. There were coke fires in those days and he was responsible for looking after them and putting the dough in. That was a heavy job. I think he worked till he was sixty-seven. My da and Paddy Hagan were thick as thieves. Argyle House was McGrath's Bar then. You'd find them in there nearly every Saturday night, Paddy Hagan, my father Dick, Alec Burnside, John Hume (John's father), a whole clique of them, sitting, sipping and talking. I used to go in as well. I remember one Saturday near the end of the night, I was going to get a round - it was my turn - and my da said "*Billy, you're only a labourer*". I was an electrician's mate at the time. He said "*I'm a tradesman, I'll get this*". It turns out I was working a forty-eight hour week. My da was working a sixty hour week. I was working in the old Londonderry Electric Light Station and I had twelve shillings a week more than my father. My da and Paddy Hagan were neighbours. They worked together and they socialised together. My da was in a couple of wee football teams back in the 1920's and earlier. He ran a couple of football teams too. There were a lot of competitions. He enjoyed a bottle of stout, he loved the horses, and he loved the Brandywell. Every Saturday he went down the town in the morning to do the horses. Then over to the Brandywell in the afternoon, home for his tea, up to McGraths then down from McGraths about half ten and that was it. *That was the life my uncles never had.*

Billy's father and mother, Dick and Mary Anne, pictured at Bundoran fifty odd years ago.

My father never talked about his loss. He never went to the War Memorial. Armistice Day was a bad day. On Armistice Day he did nothing. Before we had TV, my mother listened to the service on the wireless but not my father. He was hurt. He was never involved in the British Legion, nor the Legion with him. The names of his four brothers are on the War Memorial. His four brothers are all looking down Butcher Street. I never heard him talking or bragging about the war or what he'd done or what they'd done or anything else."

Top: My grandfather, Frederick Slater, fourth from left, pictured during a break from military training in Aldershot.

Above: Fragment of a postcard sent from Aldershot by Frederick Slater to his girlfriend, Lizzie Goligher.

Right: Lilian Mildred Slater, Frederick's and Lizzie's only daughter.

Lorraine Smyth remembers

Frederick Slater

Frederick Slater, born in 1886 in Swindon, Wiltshire, was my maternal grandfather. He was the son of Thomas Slater and Sarah Ann Gillet of Elstow, Bedfordshire. Frederick was a career soldier and met my grandmother, Elizabeth Goligher, as far as we are aware, when he was stationed in Ireland. In the pre-war years, my grandfather was a reserve in the Army and worked for Messrs. Miller & Beatty, Bishop Street, Londonderry.

He was called up at the outbreak of war and, on 27th August 1914, sailed to France with the British Expeditionary Force leaving behind his wife and baby daughter, Lilian Mildred, who was named after his only sister. My mother was to be his only child and from the few precious photographs that we have of our grandfather, the likeness between them is striking. Like so many other soldiers, he was never to return to his family as he was wounded on 30th April 1915 at Hill 60 during the second Battle of Ypres. According to my mother, her father was a stretcher bearer and was shot by a sniper while carrying out his duty on the battlefield. He then was taken to a field hospital where he died, on 3rd May 1915, from his wounds.

Frederick was buried in Balleuil Cemetery on the Belgian border with France. Our family feel that we are blessed in that we know where our grandfather's remains lie. My mother, all

KILLED IN ACTION.

Slater—Killed in action, with the British Expeditionary Force in France, on 30th April, 1915, Corporal F. C. Slater, 1st Hampshire Regiment, Beloved husband of Mrs. Slater, Fountain-street, Londonderry.

THE DERRY STANDARD, FRIDAY MORNING, MAY 28, 1915.

ROLL OF HONOUR.

LOCAL CASUALTY LIST.

Messrs. Miller & Beatty, Derry, have been notified that one of their employees, Corporal F. C. Slater, 1st Hampshire Regiment, has been killed in action. Corporal Slater accompanied the Expeditionary Force to France in August last.

Information has been received by Mrs. M'Candless, 10, Eden-place, Derry, that her son, Private James M'Candless, 1st Battalion Royal Inniskilling Fusiliers, has been wounded at the Dardanelles.

The relatives of Private P. Donnelly, 2nd Battalion Royal Inniskilling Fusiliers, who reside at 21, Brandywell-avenue, Londonderry, have received information that he has been seriously wounded by an explosive bullet, and is at present in Highfield Hospital, where he is undergoing four operations.

Example of the dripfeed of news in the local press from the battlefields of Flanders and the Dardanelles.

her life, had a deep sense of loss at not having the privilege of knowing her father and her dearest wish was that she or someone in the family could find and visit his final resting place.

After a lot of research, my sister, Colette Deeney, was able to get the information about where the cemetery and grave are located. Unfortunately, my mother was not well enough to travel overseas, at that time, so my sister and her husband, Kevin, made the pilgrimage to France on the family's behalf. After their return, my mother was then able to see photographs of her father's grave and also touch the clay and pebbles that covered him. This trip proved to be a very emotional journey for all concerned. This was something that gave my mother closure and, in turn, gave us - her children - great pleasure. We realise that we are very fortunate as a lot of families have not been that lucky. My mother had a large family of twelve children and named her second son, Frederick, after her father. She had in her possession medals and a 'cap badge' which belonged to her father and shortly

My sister, Colette, at the grave of our grandfather

before her death, my mother entrusted Frederick with these precious gifts which he will always treasure.

My grandmother, Elizabeth, had moved from Foyleview, off Foyle Road, and was living at Fountain Street, Londonderry when she got the news of Frederick's death.

My grandmother remarried, to a man called McDermott around 1927. They made their new home in Pitt Street. My older brothers and sisters can clearly remember being in this little house and playing with a 'big chest' in the loft which we always thought belonged to Frederick. Inside this trunk, my brother can remember seeing a cut throat razor with a mother of pearl handle. My sister Marie recalls reading a tiny little bible.

After her second husband died, Elizabeth moved to England but returned soon after and lived at my mother's home in Wellington Street for some time. She secured a place in Melrose House in the Waterside area of the city in the early 1950's and lived there, very happily, to the ripe old age of eighty-five. She was, until her death, a member of the Ladies Orange Order and her collarette is framed and proudly displayed at my sister Colette's home. My grandmother died on 12th December 1970. She is buried at the City Cemetery and her funeral was conducted from my mother's home in the Creggan Estate. The service was attended by a lot of her close friends and her minister officiated at the house and at the graveside.

The family has had a tradition since we were children of visiting the War Memorial in the Diamond and seeking our grandfather's name there. This has been carried on over the years with his grandchildren and now his great-grandchildren.

I grew up with a Protestant and a Catholic grandmother. It was a liberal upbringing with respect on both sides."

Geraldine and Jim O'Neill remember

Patrick and John Heaney

Geraldine O'Neill

" I was aware for quite a number of years that my grandfather's name, Patrick Heaney, was recorded on the Diamond War Memorial and brought people to look at it. He came from 56, King Street in the Waterside. My initial contact was with the late Jim Guy who was going out to visit the battlefields and graves in France and Belgium. I gave him Patrick Heaney's name and asked him if he could try to locate my grandfather's grave.

When he came back, he rang me to say that he had managed to locate the grave and he also gave me Patrick's number and details. He then said there was another person from 56 King Street listed and that his name was John Heaney. I knew this must have been my great-uncle. I discovered later that John Heaney was killed in May 1915 and my grandfather was killed in July 1916. From what I can gather, John never married. He died a young man in his early twenties. His name is also recorded on the War Memorial.

Some years later, in 2008, myself, my son Jim, who has always been interested in the family history and my daughter Deirdre, decided to go and see the graves. A friend who lives in Kent drove us over to France. By then I knew from local historian Trevor Temple that John didn't

Jim O'Neill and his mother, Geraldine, at the Diamond War Memorial. (Photograph courtesy of Jackie McColgan, Yes! Publications)

have a grave. His body was never found and so his name was inscribed upon a memorial. When we found my grandfather's grave, I placed a plant there in remembrance and we took photographs. Then we went on to find John's name on the list of people who had died. John was a member of the Inniskilling Fusiliers and we had a lot of information from the Inniskilling Fusiliers. We were

MEMORIAL REGISTER.

The whole of this Form should be filled up to the RIGHT OF CENTRAL LINE
and returned as early as possible to the address printed on the back.

PLEASE WRITE CLEARLY.

Surname	HEANEY
Rank	Private
Christian or Forenames (in full)	Patrick
Regimental Number	21959.
Military Honours	
Particulars of Company, Battery, etc., and, in case of Naval Units, the name of the Ship should be given	8th Battalion
Regiment	Royal Irish Fusiliers
Nature of death (if desired and if particulars are available)	Died of wounds.
Date of death	21st July 1916.
Native place of deceased (if not a native of Londonderry state connection with City)	Place of Birth unknown over 40 years a resident of Derry.
Any other particulars in reference to Soldier (if desired)	

PLEASE WRITE CLEARLY.

(Signed) Annie Heaney.   Relationship Wife

Address 56 King St. Waterside Londonderry.

w2684

Heaney family applications to
the Londonderry Corporation
requesting that the names of
Patrick (pictured above) and
his younger brother, John, be
recorded on the Diamond War
Memorial. (Photograph
courtesy of Brian Irwin).

REGISTER.

to the RIGHT OF CENTRAL LINE
printed on the back.

PLEASE WRITE CLEARLY.

Surname	Heaney
Rank	Private
Christian or Forenames (in full) ...	John
Regimental Number	3814.
Military Honours	
Particulars of Company, Battery, etc., and, in case of Naval Units, the name of the Ship should be given	2nd Battalion
Regiment	Royal Inniskilling Fusiliers
Nature of death (if desired and if particulars are available)	Killed in action
Date of death	16/5/1915.
Native place of deceased (if not a native of Londonderry state connection with City)	Glendermott. I.M.R.
Any other particulars in reference to Soldier (if desired)	

PLEASE WRITE CLEARLY.

(Signed) Bridget Heaney   Relationship Sister

Address 56 King St. Waterside Londonderry.

w2684

able to search his name on the regimental Memorial Wall. We also found his name in the Book of Remembrance.

They had died roughly within a year of each other. The memorial for John is about two miles away from where Patrick is buried - a five-minute drive apart. It was a very sombre and poignant occasion in the graveyard. Such a huge number of sixteen and seventeen year olds ... boys ... and we may have been the first ones ever to visit these graves.

When I look back, it is strange that we didn't know all along about my great-uncle John because I visited my grandmother nearly every week. I remember her bringing out the papers connected with my grandfather's grave and photographs of where he was buried that were probably sent after he died. We also had a great-aunt, Bridget, who lived in the family home. She was their sister. She never married and she always lived there with my grandmother. But there was never any mention of the other brother. We were children at the time, admittedly, but there was no mention of John and I have a fairly good memory. I don't understand it.

My grandmother died when we were young children and Aunt Bridget died a couple of years later.

I worked on the family tree and found out that the Heaney's came from Cloughcor in Tyrone. I had planned to go to the graveyard in Cloughcor to find out if any family were buried there but discovered that when my great-grandfather was sixty-six years of age and my great-grandmother roughly the same age, they came to live in King Street.

My grandfather got married on Christmas Day 1900. I don't know if he was a regular soldier already in the army when the war started. By coincidence I was married on Boxing Day. My grandmother's maiden name was Annie Duffy and she came from Enagh Lough in the Waterside. Patrick was the eldest and of course he had his father's name, as was common then. In the 1911 Census Patrick is described as '*a labourer*'. I have a feeling that John was too young in 1914. I wonder about Patrick's motivation. There was no conscription. He didn't have to join up. He was a father of five. His sister Bridget was living in the house and would have been a good help with the five children. It's difficult to know the reasons. His motivation must have been quite high. All those soldiers from Ireland - it was voluntary - their own choosing, they weren't pushed into it.

My own father was John Heaney. I imagine he was called after his dead uncle John. My Aunt Annie was the first to leave to go to England and maybe she got the papers after my grandmother died. She would know what happened to the medals and the Death Penny. Annie was very close to my grandmother. My grandmother Heaney was a very quiet person. I suppose when there were two people killed, it was a subject she didn't want to dwell on."

Jim O'Neill

" We are each a product of our history in some ways but how we embrace that is up to each of us. Growing up I wasn't aware I had any relatives in the First World War. The First World War was completely foreign to me. Partly it seemed something from another culture. Working now with other communities, it becomes clear that we have more in common than we realise. No matter what our cultural background, when we explore beneath the surface, we are very similar.

It's exciting to be able to pass this story on to the next generation. They'll grow up knowing about their ancestors, knowing that my great-grandfather and my great grand-uncle both fought and died in the First World War. There has been a growing change in attitudes about the First World War within the Nationalist community over the last ten years but also within the Unionist community in relation to the Irish involvement in that war. Recently I was talking to a local politician who is very involved in the Messines Project. He said that he hadn't realised Nationalists had fought in such numbers in the First World War.

Some years ago when I studied history, a gifted teacher both brought the subject alive and helped break down some myths. He talked about the Battle of the Boyne and told us that Pope Alexander VIII celebrated King William's defeat of King James. He talked too about the 1916 Rising when the rebels, arrested by the British, were spat at and jeered by the local people. It was only after their execution by the British Army that the leaders of the Rising were hailed as heroes. History needs to be untangled from mythology."

Kate de Louvois, Marion Ross, Linda Ross and Anne McCartney remember

Robert and James McNulty

Kate de Louvois

"When my aunt Matilda died in Exeter, her son, George, let me go through her old photographs and among them was a remembrance card for Robert McNulty. Something in his face and features drew me to him and I realised that here was a man, a family member, I knew absolutely nothing about. I had never even known of his existence. I suddenly became aware that I wanted to do something to remember him and to make sure that the rest of the family also knew about him.

Robert was my grandmother's brother, my great-uncle. He was one of two brothers who fought in the First World War. Robert was killed on 16 May, 1915 and then James, his brother, suffered the same fate a few months later on 15 August, 1915. I imagined it must have been devastating for the family to lose two sons in quick succession. I undertook then to create a family tree and to incorporate everything I knew about Robert and James

Robert McNulty, killed on 16th May, 1915.

into it so that the rest of the family became aware of them. This was a big learning experience for me. I began to make so many contacts with the rest of my family here. It's been a very positive process of discovery and re-connecting.

Robert and James were the sons of Robert and Matilda (née Gallagher) McNulty. There were also two girls in the family: my grandmother, Mary Elizabeth and Sarah Ann. At one time the family lived in Greenslades Row which doesn't exist any more. Other records point to them living at various other locations in the Wapping Lane area. Their mother, Matilda, died in late January, 1903. On November 24th of the same year, Robert remarried, to Maggie McElwee. He had another son, Mark, who was born at the end of 1904.

When I think back to the picture of my great-uncle Robert there was something very haunting about him. He seemed almost to be calling out to me. Growing up we were never told about Robert or James. We weren't told that they are remembered on the War Memorial in the Diamond ... the number of times I have walked past it, unaware that my two great-uncles were part of it. Robert married Mary Ann Clarke on 3 February, 1913 and he joined the 2nd Battalion, Royal Inniskilling Fusiliers at the onset of war in 1914. He served in France and Belgium and subsequently lost his life during the battle of Festubert. He is buried at the Guards' Cemetery, Windy Corner, Cuinchy, France. He was 21 years old."

Linda Ross

A few years ago, I became aware of our cousin Kate's research and immediately contacted her as I had always been very interested in my family history. As a child I was aware of my grandfather James's death at Gallipoli because my father had often spoke of it and taken me to visit the War Memorial, where his name is recorded. It always struck me as very poignant that we didn't know anything about the other members of my father's family. In particular, we never knew that James had a brother who was also killed in the First World War, even though their names appear, side by side, on the War Memorial.

As a history graduate I had already begun to delve into the circumstances surrounding the catastrophic events that had unfolded in Gallipoli and had found references to my grandfather's name in various casualty lists compiled during the campaign. When Kate forwarded her research material to me, it re-awakened my interest and thus began our correspondence. In particular, I was also deeply affected by the photograph of Robert who bore a remarkable resemblance to my son, Graeme, and to my father as well. My father was the only son of James and Sarah (nee Orr) McNulty of 6 Charlotte Street, Londonderry and he had a younger sister, Eileen. James and Sarah were married on 9 May 1911 and my father, also named James, was born on 29 November, 1912. I remember thinking how sad it was that my father had never really known his immediate family as, after his father was killed in 1915, his mother and sister went to live in England, leaving him in the care of his maternal grandparents and he was never to live with his mother and sister again. We suspect that the schism in the family occurred because of the circumstances surrounding James and Sarah's marriage. It had been a mixed marriage. James was a Catholic and Sarah a Protestant. They had been married for four years and he was just 26 years old when he was killed."

Anne McCartney

When Kate sent us her research I was struck by how little I actually knew about my father's family. He rarely talked about them and there were only a few photographs but, certainly, none of my grandfather or his brother. Indeed, as a child, I was unaware that he had a brother. I knew that my grandfather had been killed at Gallipoli but the First World War seemed so distant and I had little curiosity about it at that time. In recent years I have learned more about the horror and human cost of that war. It was Trevor Temple who told me that my grandfather had died in the battle of Suvla Bay and explained that the Irish Division landed on the 7 August 1915; they were not given any orders to advance immediately but were kept on the ridge for a whole week with very little water or food; this crucial delay allowed the Turks to bring in reinforcements. Those who weren't slaughtered on the ridge, died of infection. My grandfather's body was never found but his name is on the Helles Memorial in Turkey. I had never heard of Suvla Bay before but learned that it does feature in several songs such as Eric Bogle's 'And the Band Played Waltzing Matilda' which mentions '*the blood stained sands … And how in that hell, that they*

Sepia ink image on leaf created by Marion Ross

called Suvla Bay, we were butchered like lambs at the slaughter'. Knowing how much my grandfather suffered and the sheer waste of his life brought him closer to me and made me think of all the other untold stories within my family circle - of the father whose two sons were killed within the same year; of the bereaved wives who were left to rear their families; of my grandmother who left for England, taking her daughter but leaving behind her only son and, of that son - our father, who never lived with his mother again."

Marion Ross

" When I first saw the photograph of my great-uncle Robert, I was intrigued by it because he bore such a strong resemblance to my own father … and also to my nephew, Graeme. I kept the photograph in my study and, last year, whilst I was studying for a degree in fine and applied arts and exploring the theme of memory and identity, I knew I had to use it in some way. His face fascinated me. I can't really explain why. I found it extremely haunting and so very poignant. The family resemblance was quite amazing. I remember taking an acetate photocopy of Robert's photograph and placing it over a photograph I had of Graeme and it was as if they were one image: their features, the shape of their face, their hair-line, even their eye-brows were all uncannily similar.

'Soliloquy' by Marion Ross

I drew portrait after portrait of Robert, some in sepia ink, others in charcoal and pencil and, even though I explored other family connections and resemblances in relation to my theme, I kept returning to my great-uncle Robert and the First World War. A part of my past had become palpably available to me. Robert's image allowed me, possibly, for the first time, to think of my grandfather, James, as a real person who, together with his brother, had belonged to that vast body of invisible young men, the unknown soldiers sent from all over Europe who had fought and *'die[d] as cattle'* as Wilfred Owen described it.

I created a series of paintings, a personal and imaginative evocation of the First World War. In one of these I incorporated an acetate image taken from Robert's photograph and because words are very important to me, I decided to insert an epitaph I had chanced upon. Written in 1915 by H. W. Garrod, a Fellow of Merton College, Oxford, and one of the many wartime imitations of Simonides' ancient epitaph on Thermoplyae, *Epitaph: Neuve Chapelle* is very simple but, to me, it says all there is to say about the First World War:

> *'Tell them at home, there's nothing here to hide:*
> *We took our orders, asked no questions, died.'*

In another work, I again combined the visual and the verbal by featuring the names of First World War battles, including the battles of Festubert and Gallipoli where Robert and James had perished. I also painted a rather unconventional portrait of Robert. There is something about that face - so handsome, so innocent, so heartrendingly young - I needed to portray how war had destroyed lives and decimated families.

Finally, I painted images in sepia ink on leaves, some of them oak leaves (referring to Doire - the place of the oak). I found that people were very moved by these leaf paintings. Intimations of loss, disintegration, decay and the identification of fallen leaves with fallen lives obviously spring to mind but, they also convey a sense of place and memory, two key aspects of identity. And, on reflection, it is in terms of identity that the research initiated by Kate and my subsequent exploration of it through the medium of art, has proved to be immensely enriching to me. A few more pieces of the incomplete jigsaw that comprises my identity have slotted into place and some of the enigmas that permeated my childhood have, undoubtedly, found resolution."

Installation of the Diamond War Memorial, June 1927.
(Photograph courtesy of the Bigger McDonald Collection).

Clive Johnston remembers

James Holmes
and John Short Haslett

James Holmes Haslett and below, John Short Haslett

" My interest in the First World War stems from the fact that my two great-uncles, James Holmes Haslett and his brother John Short Haslett, both reared in Clooney Terrace in the Waterside, lost their lives during that war. This interest was initially sparked off by a chance finding in my mother's attic of a typewritten letter from a L/Corporal Albert Beech sent from Gallipoli in 1915. This letter was sent to her grandparents in Clooney Terrace and it related to the death of their eldest son James Holmes Haslett killed on 9 August 1915 while serving with the Australian Army Medical Corps in Gallipoli as a stretcher bearer.

L/Corporal Beech wrote that he was a friend of Holmes from before the war and was with him when he died. I imagine that it was comforting for his parents to know he didn't die alone fighting with a strange army in a strange country. Captain Conerick, the unit's medical officer, also attended Holmes while he died. Conerick was the medical officer of the Brisbane Athletic Club where Holmes trained. He also wrote to Holmes' parents.

Holmes' younger brother John was killed the following year at the Somme on 1 July. His body was never recovered. Holmes is buried in Beach Cemetery in Gallipoli with a fine headstone and flowers. John has his name on Thiepval Memorial. I feel a sense of family duty to ensure that neither are forgotten. I'm coming to an age now where I'm thinking about the next generation. I have one son and

GALLIPOLI,

14th November, 1915.

Dear Mr. & Mrs. Haslett :-

You will, no doubt, have heard the
sad news of your brave son Jim.   I am writing as one of his old
pals and mates.   We joined Camp together in Queensland, and was
mates all through.   He was one of the bravest and best men that
ever stepped foot on Gallipoli.   He landed on Gallipoli with me
the morning of the 25th of April.   You will have heard of the
landing on Gallipoli, no doubt.

Well, Mrs. Haslett, poor old Jim was never afraid of anything.   He would go anywhere.   He was in my Stretcher squad, and
Jimmie would do anything for me.   I was one of the ones to pick
him up, and take him to the Dressing Station, and the
last words he said was, "Hurry up, Bert".   This is my Christian
name (Bert).   He knew me right up to the last.   There is one
thing, we were all thankful he was not knocked about.   He only
had the one bullet mark in the right shoulder.   It sent a gloom
over the whole of the Camp.   He was greatly missed.

I am sending you a cutting of poor old Jim's Photo out of one
of the Queensland papers, so I sincerely hope you will get it safely.
It is pretty much like him, and there is one thing you can always
be proud of, that is for his giving his country.   He was attending to
a wounded soldier and a shell burst over him, and one pellet struck
him on the shoulder, and he died about half-an-hour after.   No doubt
you will have been notified of your dear son's death long before
this.   I would have written earlier, only I was waiting for a
Photo of his Grave to send it to you.   I have not received it yet,
but will send it as soon as I get it.   I know you will be very
pleased to get it.   You will be able probably to get the Photo
enlarged.   So now, Mrs. Haslett, I hope you will cheer up, as you

now

<u>know</u> your brave dear son died a hero for his King and Country.
He was well liked by all who knew him.   They all thought the
world of Jimmie.   So now Mrs. Haslett and family I will close.
Wishing you all a Merry Christmas and a Prosperous New Year.   I
would like very much to receive a short letter from you, so as I
will know you have received the photo.   So Good bye.

I must humbly apologise for not writing to you sooner, as I
wanted to give the Military Authorities time to let you know, and
also to get the Photo of your dearly beloved son James.

I remain,

Yours truly,

No. 28, Lance Corporal Beech,

A Section,

A. I. F.,

GALLIPOLI.

Kindly accept our deepest sympathy for your late beloved
son James, who was dearly loved by all his comrades, as he
was a great favourite in the Corps.

Yours sincerely,

MEMBERS of the

3rd Field Ambulance.

if I don't put these stories of the previous generation together maybe nobody ever will. My mother is the brothers' closest living relative. She is eighty-eight and her excellent memory has been very helpful in my research.

When I was a youngster visiting my grandmother's house with my sister, I had a vague awareness of my great-uncles because I used to play with the two bronze memorial plaques or "Death Pennies". My grandmother, a sister to Holmes and John, never spoke much about them.

In family memory, James Holmes Haslett was tall, good-looking, athletic, and dynamic. My mother told me that when Holmes finished school, he worked in Bank Place in a wholesale grocery store and that he used to practice for long distance running by racing the mail boat from Derry to Moville. Apparently he was very well known in the local sports scene both as a long distance runner

James Holmes Haslett's original grave at Gallipoli

and also as a boxer. I heard recently that he was to box in the Guildhall, prize fighting for a guinea. Somebody came into the family shop on Clooney Terrace to wish him luck in the fight. When his father, John, a very strict Presbyterian, heard this, he was horrified at the thought of his son boxing for money. He proposed that *"he would give Holmes the guinea for not boxing."* In 1910, Holmes emigrated to Sydney to run in the Sydney Marathon and family history records that he won it. He then moved to Brisbane to work as a salesman and, while he was there, he joined the Queensland Voluntary Ambulance Unit. He also involved himself in the Brisbane Athletic Club where Captain Conerick was medical officer.

When war broke out in 1914, the Queensland Ambulance Unit joined the Australian Army Medical Unit en masse. Australian soldiers and the Medical Corps with Holmes on board then set sail from Brisbane to go to England, thinking they were on their way to France. Instead they were diverted to Egypt when the War Council decided to invade the Dardanelles. In Gallipoli on August 9th 1915, a shell exploded overhead and Holmes was struck in the right shoulder. A piece of shrapnel partially severed his spinal cord. Half an hour later he died in the medical station.

I have a childhood memory of my grandmother telling me that she had intercepted the postman coming along Clooney Terrace with the telegram telling of Holmes' death. She saw him coming up the street and just knew he was coming to their house. She gave the telegram to her parents.

They hadn't seen their son since 1910. The following year, she saw the postman coming again to say that John Short Haslett had been killed at the Somme. She hid this telegram for two days before she could bring herself to give it to her parents.

My grandmother was widowed twice. Both marriages lasted only a few years. My grandmother was on her own then for many, many years. She was a very kind, generous woman but never talked about her personal life. She rarely talked about her brothers. She would deflect the conversation away. It was only later that I realised, through my mother, how deeply hurt my grandmother had been at the loss of Holmes and John. Particularly at the loss of John who wasn't quite so independent and was closer in age to her. My grandmother didn't attend any remembrance services or church services or go to the Diamond on Remembrance Sunday. There is a memorial in Ebrington Church but she never referred to that either. She was stoic and kept her memories to herself.

Her father originally had a drapery shop in Bonds Street (which is now a taxi and cycle place). They lived at 14 Clooney Terrace. Then in 1908, he bought 37 Clooney Terrace, (which is now Clooney Meats), and set up a grocery and hardware store there. He was an elder in Waterside Presbyterian Church and became one of the founder elders of the new Ebrington Presbyterian Church at May Street on Limavady Road which was built to cope with increasing numbers of Presbyterians in the area. Ebrington Presbyterian Church opened in 1897. James Holmes Haslett, the eldest son, had been baptised in the Waterside

Hannah Haslett, mother of Holmes and John.

Hannah May Haslett (May), sister to Holmes and John Haslett and grandmother of Clive Johnston.

Presbyterian Church. John, the second son, was one of the first children to be baptised in the new Ebrington Presbyterian Church. The third Haslett child was Margaret Elizabeth - known as Lizzie. She later married Samuel Hamilton and they had a farm at Campsie. My grandmother was the fourth child. She was christened Hannah May, although she hated that name and she was known as May.

My mother (May's daughter) was born in 1921 and never knew her two uncles. She was an only child and was partially reared by her grandparents in Clooney Terrace. She went to school on Clooney Terrace and was married in Waterside Presbyterian Church. My father was a policeman in Derry during the Second World War. Because we are a police family, we lived all over Northern Ireland. When my father was serving, I don't remember him going to Remembrance Sunday ceremonies. I have done so since I was a schoolboy, and still do. One day when I was well into my marriage, I had my parents up in Derry. We were doing a nostalgic walk around the city and my father said to me at the Diamond, "There's your two uncles' names." I got a bit of a shiver. Although I knew of their existence, I had never thought of them being commemorated. Some years later I took my son to see Holmes and John's names on the War Memorial.

In some ways, I'm quite impersonal about my two great-uncles. I think over what they must have gone through but I am not maudlin about them. I don't think *"What a ghastly tragedy. How might life have been different if this hadn't happened?"* They are ancestors rather than people I grew up with or knew. I honour their name and I'm astounded by their bravery. I am proud to have two uncles who went out, without hesitation, fought and died.

I have been able to track down so much information about James Holmes Haslett and it has been a struggle to discover more about John. Through research in the Central Library and copies of the Sentinel showing his death notice, I found out that John Short Haslett worked as a clerk in the Belfast Shipping Company in Londonderry. I discovered too that he had attended Ebrington National School and the Model School in Northland Road.

Towards the end of my grandmother's life, when she was going into sheltered housing, my mother went to visit her. She found her mother sitting by the fire, taking her old sepia photographs from a biscuit tin, tearing them in two and burning them. Because she was such a private person, she didn't want them seen by anyone in the care home where she was going. Now there are only a few photographs existing of all that family history from the 1880's, 1890's, right through to the 1950's, 1960's. In my grandmother's cabinet there were also the two bronze memorial plaques for Holmes and John. Those never made the move to the care home either. She must have disposed of them somehow rather than let anybody else get them. She had kept the photographs and the Death Pennies right up until the 1960's or 1970's. Then, when she no longer had a place of her own, she saw fit to dispose of everything. It wasn't through shame or guilt or sorrow. She had her memories and they were private. I find that very poignant.

When I unearthed information about the lives of James Holmes Haslett and John Short Haslett, I reproduced each item to show to my mother. She was touched. She told me: *"What you have produced here, your grandmother never knew. She never knew where her brother Holmes was buried. She never would have seen that grave, never would have known where the battle was. She would never have known any of his life in Brisbane or what ship he sailed in with the Australian Forces. She would have known nothing about that at all. Isn't it remarkable that ninety years later you can find all this information, stories, photographs and everything."* There was a catch in her voice. *"I would just love your grandmother to have seen this."*

I feel now that I have brought these two dead men out of history where they were fading away to nothing. I have ensured that they will not be forgotten.

Postscript

All along I had thought that John Haslett Junior (John Short Haslett's nephew), was dead but I was pleased to find that I was wrong. I arranged to visit him last year. He is an amazing man. Still working a six day week at seventy-nine years of age. We had a wonderful chat together. He had the finest china out and he entertained me royally. I asked him did anybody ever tell him how John had died? He told me that John was a grenade thrower - with the Tenth Battalion, that he had a lot of grenades on a belt and when he pulled one off, they all fell off and the pins came out. He was emotional when he was telling me this and yet he didn't know if that was actually the way it happened. That was just what he remembered being told. We were more or less finished our conversation and I was noting down all the titbits of memories he had, when he said "Hold on a minute, Clive, till we see. My wife has a wee jewellery box". He came back with a box of her rings and brooches and in it was John's Victory Medal, no ribbon on it, just a pink bow attached to it. But nonetheless John Haslett's Victory Medal. I was so amazed and then he gave it to me. I took it home and put a fresh ribbon on it."

"YOUR FIRST DUTY
IS TO TAKE YOUR PART IN
ENDING
THE WAR"

Mr. J. E. REDMOND, M.P.
at Waterford 23rd August 1915.

JOIN AN
IRISH REGIME
TO-DAY

The glamour of recruitment posters
concealed the horror of war.

Don't be Alarmed
the
Royal Irish
are
"On Guard"
at
FERMOY.

39916

WE ARE DOING
OUR DUTY AT LONDONDERRY

THOUGH DUTY TOOK ME FROM YOUR SIDE,
AT THE EMPIRE'S CALL TO FIGHT;
THERE'S NONE CAN EVER LOVE YOU MORE,
THAN HE WHO WRITES TO-NIGHT.

Michael Doherty remembers
John Doherty

" My great grand-uncle was John Doherty. Even though he was reared in a Republican family very much opposed to British rule in Ireland, John Doherty, as a young man, joined the British Army. John was killed at Loos. His name is inscribed upon the Cenotaph in the Diamond.

A line drawing by Michael Doherty created during his visit to the battlefields of France and Belgium in 2005.

For more than twenty years now, I have been involved in community relations work. Three years ago I was working with a group of Loyalists. We were sharing our thoughts about the Battle of the Somme and the 1916 Rising. One of the group members, a loyalist ex-prisoner, told me that he was going to visit the Somme the following year. When he invited me to come along, I accepted the invitation.

Later that same week I was over in my father's house chatting. I told him that I was going to visit the Somme. He was half reading the newspaper. He looked over the top of the paper and told me, for the first time, that my great-great uncle, John Doherty had gone to fight in the First World War and had been killed. He told me that when the telegram came in January 1916 to tell the family that John Doherty had been killed, his father, Manasses Doherty, burned the telegram and expressly forbade the family ever to mention John again. My father had never spoken about John Doherty to me until that moment. That night, we had a long conversation about our family's history, about Republicanism and about how strongly our family opposed the British presence in Ireland. My father's understanding was that when John Redmond had called for Irish Nationalists to volunteer for the British Army and fight for "the freedom of small nations," John Doherty had heeded this call and enlisted. To my father, John Doherty was a Redmondite.

With the help of local historian Trevor Temple, I discovered that John Doherty served with the Royal Irish Regiment and was with the Sixth Battalion. Apparently he enlisted at Templemore, 'within the city and county of Londonderry.' My hunch is that he joined up thinking that if Britain won the war, then Ireland would become free. Within my family circle, even joining 'Redmond's army' was still joining the British Army. Here was a young

DEATH OF MR. MANASSES DOHERTY

A very old member of the Londonderry printing business has passed away in Mr. Manasses Doherty. For over half-a-century he was in the employment of the "Derry Journal." A strong Nationalist, he figured in many a stirring scene in the old days. But it was his characteristic that he never allowed party feeling to interfere with private friendships.

MEMORIAL REGISTER.

The whole of this Form should be filled up to the RIGHT OF CENTRAL LINE
and returned as early as possible to the address printed on the back.

PLEASE WRITE CLEARLY.

Surname	Doherty,
Rank	Private
Christian or Forenames (in full)	John
Regimental Number	2407,
Military Honours	
Particulars of Company, Battery, etc., and, in case of Naval Units, the name of the Ship should be given	6ᵗʰ Batt (Irish Brigade)
Regiment	Royal Irish Regiment
Nature of death (if desired and if particulars are available)	Killed in Action at Hill 70. Loos France
Date of death	21st January, 1916.
Native place of deceased (if not a native of Londonderry state connection with City)	X Londonderry IHR
Any other particulars in reference to Soldier (if desired)	

PLEASE WRITE CLEARLY.

(Signed) *Sarah Doherty*   Relationship *Mother*

Address *133 Lecky Road*

Londonderry

w2266

In spite of her husband, Manasses' interdict, John Doherty's mother, Sarah, made application to the Londonderry Corporation for her son's name to be recorded on the Diamond War Memorial.

CENSUS OF IRELAND, 1911.

No. on Form B. 133

Two Examples of the mode of filling up this Table are given on the other side.

FORM A.

RETURN of the MEMBERS of this FAMILY and their VISITORS, BOARDERS, SERVANTS, &c., who slept or abode in this House on the night of SUNDAY, the 2nd of APRIL, 1911.

No.	NAME AND SURNAME (Christian Name)	NAME AND SURNAME (Surname)	RELATION to Head of Family.	RELIGIOUS PROFESSION.	EDUCATION.	AGE (Males)	AGE (Females)	RANK, PROFESSION, OR OCCUPATION.	PARTICULARS AS TO MARRIAGE (Whether "Married," "Widower," "Widow," or "Single.")	Completed years the present Marriage has lasted.	Total Children born alive.	Children still living.	WHERE BORN.	IRISH LANGUAGE.	If Deaf and Dumb, &c.
1	Manasses	Doherty	Head of Family	Roman Catholic	Read and write	59		Printer – compositor	Married	35	13	13	New Zealand	Irish & English	
2	Sarah	Doherty	Wife	"	"		53		"	35	13	13	"		
3	Constantine	Doherty	Son	"	"	34		monoto–compositor (unemployed)	Single				"	Irish & English	
4	Patrick	Doherty	Son	"	"	32		Printer-compositor	"				"	Irish & English	
5	Sarah	Doherty	Daughter	"	"		26	Seamstress	"				"		
6	Jenny	Doherty	Daughter	"	"		21	Seamstress	"				"		
7	Thomas	Doherty	Son	"	"	19		Painter	"				"		
8	John	Doherty	Son	"	"	17		Barber	"				"		
9	Maggie	Doherty	Daughter	"	"		15	Seamstress	"				"	Irish & English	
10	Josephine	Doherty	Daughter	"	"		13	Scholar	"				"	Irish & English	
11	Roddy	Doherty	Son	"	"	9		Scholar	"				"	Irish & English	
12															
13	Edward	McBride	Lodger	Roman Catholic	"	45		Butcher	"				"	Irish & English	
14															
15															

I hereby certify, as required by the Act 10 Edw. VII., and 1 Geo. V., cap. 11, that the foregoing Return is correct, according to the best of my knowledge and belief.

M. Coleman   *Signature of Enumerator.*

I believe the foregoing to be a true Return.

Manasses Doherty   *Signature of Head of Family.*

Note that family members speak both Irish and English, that Manasses Doherty records his name in both Irish and English and, in a simple twist of fate, John Doherty, like Michael Doherty after him, were barbers.

man making that choice and here was his family, particularly his own father, making a decision to disown him. The Easter Rising in April 1916 and the subsequent execution of the leaders of the Rising re-inforced Irish hostility against the British at that time. I had never heard mention of John Doherty until that evening in my father's house. The process of re-discovering and accepting John Doherty had begun and I struggled to understand how Manasses Doherty could have been so cold as to disown his own flesh and blood. It is possible though that he was expressing his own grief when he destroyed that telegram. Manasses died only a few months after John in April 1916.

I had already decided I was going to the Somme when I had this conversation with my father. On that journey, a Loyalist ex-combatant, Raymond Millar and a PSNI officer found the panel where John Doherty is commemorated. I can remember Raymond running in front of me down the side of the graveyard and excitedly shouting to bring me up to it. John Doherty's name is one of many names on the panel. There is no grave. John was blown up at Loos. His body was never recovered.

Being there, I thought that I was, in all likelihood, the first person in my family circle ever to stand before that panel, to connect with that young man who died in January 1916. When I came out of the graveyard, the sun was going down. I looked across at the mountains, the coalfields and the flattened plain where the battle had taken place, I felt an amazing sense of stillness and quiet.

All this has been a journey of understanding and healing for me. Originally, I had learned about the First World War through reading and viewing DVDs. The story of John Doherty's life and death and then actually visiting the battlefields, the Memorials and the graveyards, all of these have created a new awareness.

When I became director of the Peace and Reconciliation Group, part of the group's tradition was to lay a wreath at the Cenotaph on Armistice Day. In the beginning I struggled with this. I asked myself: 'What would my father say, what would my Republican family say about me if I was seen wearing a poppy and carrying a wreath down to the Cenotaph? Would they think I was a traitor?' At the end of the day I had to make my own decision about what I was going to do. This is part of the struggle we are in at this time in Northern Ireland. How do we express who we are? After I had learned about my uncle and after I had gone to the Somme, I now lay a wreath at the Cenotaph, with meaning. Not just for the Peace and Reconciliation Group because it's their tradition. I'm doing it for John Doherty as well.

I'm now very much at peace when I walk on Remembrance Sunday. Ironically I now go to the Cenotaph twice as there is another service on the Saturday evening, the weekend previous to Remembrance Sunday. The organisation of Irish Ex-Servicemen and the British Legion have a joint remembrance ceremony. I go to that as a citizen of this city, but I don't carry a wreath. The Royal British Legion carry the Union flag and the organisation of Irish Ex-Servicemen carry the Irish Tricolour."

An extract from the Derry Journal, Monday, May 29th, 1916.

DERRY AND THE INNISKILLINGS.

CATHOLIC SOLDIERS WHO FOUGHT AND FELL.

COMRADES' ARTISTIC MEMORIAL UNVEILED.

Yesterday afternoon a beautiful ceremony took place in St. Columb's Church, Waterside when a chaste and exquisitely designed grotto of Our Lady of Lourdes, erected by Catholic soldiers belonging to the Royal Inniskilling Fusiliers stationed at Ebrington Barracks, to the memory of their fallen comrades, was unveiled. For the occasion there was a special parade of the Catholic soldiers at present at Ebrington, and they practically filled the sacred edifice and manifested a deep devotional interest in the sacred function. Rev. W. B. MacFeely, B.D., P.P., chaplain to the forces, performed the unveiling ceremony and afterwards the soldiers joined with him in reciting the rosary.

Father MacFeely then delivered an appropriate lecture in the course of which he paid eloquent tribute to the bravery of the Inniskillings, and spoke of their heroic deeds in the present great world conflict. He referred to that abiding spirit of faith characteristic of all Irishmen which the terrible realities of the war had served to bring into striking relief amongst the soldiers who had gone to do battle. Many grand manifestations of that great piety and love of faith had been provided, and it was fitting that in that church where so many brave soldiers had knelt and prayed, they should have an enduring monument to the men who fell in action. It was equally fitting that in the erection of that memorial they had found the means of doing perpetual honour to our beloved Lady of Lourdes, whose protection they should always seek, but especially in the hour of danger.

Benediction of the Most Blessed Sacrament was subsequently given by the Rev. T. Mahon, C.C., assisted by Rev. Patrick Devlin, C.C. The music incidental to the ceremonies was effectively rendered by the church choir under the capable direction of Miss E. F. Heaney, N.T. The grotto, which is the object of great admiration, is a lifelike representation of the Blessed Virgin appearing to Bernadette, and is a work of great artistic merit.

The brass plate acknowledging the role of the Royal Inniskilling Fusiliers in erecting the grotto at St. Columb's Church, Chapel Road, has long since disappeared.

APPEAL FROM

JOHN REDMOND, M.P.

To the People of Ireland.

AT the very commencement of the War I made an appeal to the Irish people, and especially to the young men of Ireland, to mark the profound change which has been brought about in the relations of Ireland to the Empire, by whole-heartedly supporting the Allies in the field.

I pointed out that, at long last, after centuries of misunderstanding, the democracy of Great Britain had finally and irrevocably decided to trust Ireland, and I called upon Ireland to prove that the concession of liberty would, as we had promised in your name, have the same effect in our country as in every other portion of the Empire, and that Ireland would henceforth be a strength, instead of a weakness.

I further pointed out that this was a just war, provoked by the intolerable military despotism of Germany; that it was a war in defence of the rights and liberties of small nationalities; and that Ireland would be false to her history and to every consideration of honour, good faith, and self-interest if she did not respond to my appeal.

I called for a distinctively Irish Army composed of Irishmen, led by Irishmen, and trained for the field at home in Ireland.

I acknowledge with profound gratitude, the magnificent response the country has made.

For the first time in history, we have to-day a huge Irish army in the field. Its achievements have covered Ireland with glory before the world, and have thrilled our hearts with pride.

North and South have vied with each other in springing to arms, and please God, the sacrifices they have made side by side on the field of battle will form the surest bond of a united Irish Nation in the future.

John Redmond appeals to the people of Ireland for further sacrifice in the cause of "a united Irish Nation."

We have kept our word. We have fulfilled our trust. We have definitely accepted the position, and undertaken the obligations of a self-governed unit amongst the nations which make up the Empire.

One more duty remains to be fulfilled. We have to stand by and maintain the Irish Army at the front.

We must not, and will not, tolerate the idea of our Irish regiments being reinforced by any but Irish soldiers. Ireland must maintain the Irish regiments until victory has been won. The gaps in the ranks of our Irish army must be filled, not by Englishmen or Scotchmen or Welshmen, but by Irishmen.

Our gallant fellow-countrymen at the front commissioned me to make this appeal.

They appeal to-day through me from the trenches to the farmers, the labourers, the artisans, and to every class of our people not to desert them.

In your name I promised them in France and Flanders that Ireland would stand by them.

Will you fulfil that promise?

The task is not difficult. Fill up the reserve battalions. Your brothers in the trenches are not only upholding the honour of Ireland before the world, they are defending Ireland itself from ruin and destruction, from murder and sacrilege, from the confiscation of the lands of the Irish farmer, and the wrecking of the property and prosperity of every class of our population.

You are under no compulsion save that of duty.

In the name of honour, justice, and religion, in the name of common gratitude, and in their own highest self-interest, I appeal to the young men of Ireland who are still available to join the Reserve Battalions, and to commence their training so that, in the event of the war not speedily ending, they may be ready to fill every gap in the ranks of "**the Irish army at the front.**"

Signed,

JOHN E. REDMOND.

17TH FEBRUARY, 1916.

SEALY, BRYERS & WALKER, PRINTERS, DUBLIN.   7380. 3/16

John Redmond's appeal is dated 17th February, 1916, two months before the Easter Rising, four months before the Battle of the Somme.

Ellen and William (Billy) Ballantine pictured together in a locket passed down through three generations of the Moore family.

.M.R.

the ... ... NTRAL LINE

and ... ... inted on the back.

CLEARLY.

Surname	BALLANTYNE
Rank	Private
Christian or Forenames (in full)	William Alexander
Regimental Number	10954
Military Honours	
Particulars of Company, Battery, etc., and, in case of Naval Units, the name of the Ship should be given	2nd Battalion
Regiment	Royal Inniskilling Fus.
Nature of death (if desired and if particulars are available)	Killed in Action.
Date of death	1st July, 1916.
Native place of deceased (if not a native of Londonderry state connection with City)	Londonderry.
Any other particulars in reference to Soldier (if desired)	

I.M.R.

PLEASE WRITE CLEARLY.

(Signed) *Margaret Moore*   Relationship *Mother in law*

Address *19 Albert Place,*   Witness

L. derry.   *Thompson*

W2266

Margaret Cockburn remembers
William (Billy) Ballantine

" My maiden name is Margaret Moore. My grandmother was Ellen Ballantine (née Moore). She married William Ballantine on 24th January 1916 in St. Columb's Cathedral. Six months later on 1st July 1916, Billy was killed at the Somme. There was incredible slaughter on that day and they never found his body.

William's name is recorded on the Thiepval Memorial and also on the War Memorial in the Diamond. His name appears on two church memorials also - in St. Columb's Cathedral and in First Derry Presbyterian Church. My grandmother belonged to the Church of Ireland and attended Derry Cathedral. William had a strong association with both churches.

I have a locket with my granny's face pictured on one side and William's on the other side. He's in his uniform. The locket must be more than ninety years old. My granny didn't wear it. It was so precious and she was too scared of losing it. She kept it upstairs.

She didn't talk a whole lot about William Ballantine. Maybe it was too hurtful to talk about him. They had only been married six months when he was killed. His death must have hit her very, very hard. She never re-married. My granny was eighty-three when she died in 1974. She was like a second mother to me.

My grandmother gave the locket to my father. When my father died, my mother had it. I was given the locket after she died. The only photograph I have of William is in that locket. There must have been old photographs of William Ballantine. I would say so, especially in his uniform. I'm sure there were others. I remember seeing photographs above the fireplace of him in his uniform and I didn't know who he was. I don't remember a Death Penny.

My granny attended the Cenotaph on Remembrance Sunday, after the Cathedral, and I'm sure she was remembering her husband. When we were wee, they didn't take us to that. They took us to church but we weren't taken to the Cenotaph. My father and my granny went as well as my Aunt Ruby and my mother. But the young ones weren't allowed to go. We wouldn't have understood anyway. You have to grow a bit to understand."

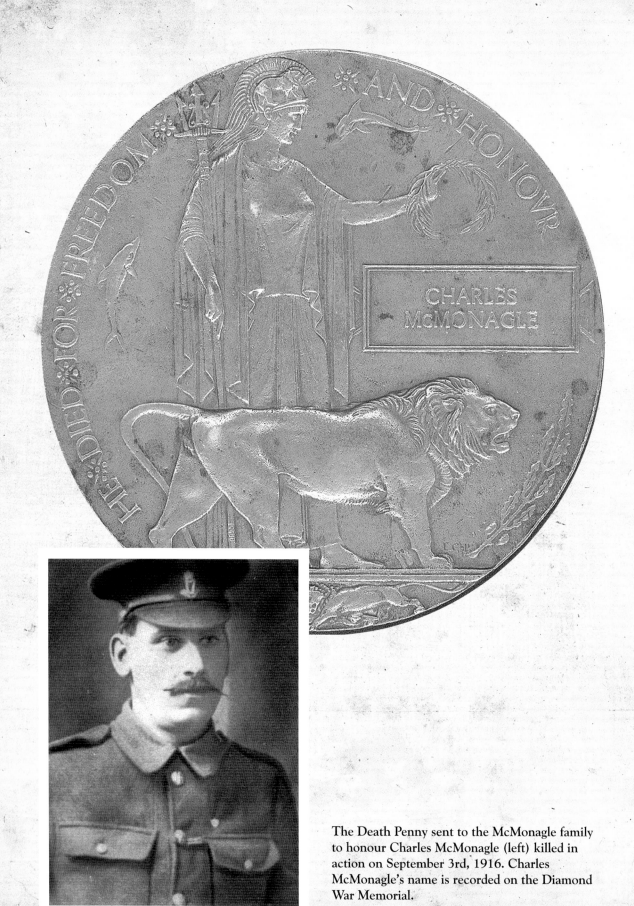

The Death Penny sent to the McMonagle family to honour Charles McMonagle (left) killed in action on September 3rd, 1916. Charles McMonagle's name is recorded on the Diamond War Memorial.

Charlie Hasson remembers

Charles McMonagle and George Hasson

" Charles McMonagle was my great grandfather on my mother's side. I'm called after both him and his eldest son Charles. Charles McMonagle was born in Fahan Street in the Bogside, grew up there and married Mary O' Neill from the same street. His older brother, Dennis McMonagle, had been in the British Army before the First World War and served in the Inniskilling Fusiliers. Around 1914 / 15 the two brothers had joined the Irish National Volunteers along with my great-grandfather's brother in law, John McMenamin, who came from the nearby St Columb's Wells. Charles and John enlisted together after Redmond made the call. They signed up in St Columb's Hall which was used as a recruiting centre for some regiments.

The two brothers went into the Royal Irish Regiment (16th Irish Division) and their brother-in-law John McMenamin went into the Inniskilling Fusiliers. They went off to the Royal Irish Regiment training camp in Fermoy and were then shipped off to England. They were at the front by late 1915 or early 1916. They didn't see much action until the Inniskillings went 'over the top' on 1 July 1916. John McMenamin was killed on the first day of the battle of the Somme.

My great-grandfather had six children. His wife had died in 1913 so he was the sole carer for the family. When he enlisted to go off to France, he left these six children behind. His sister, Catherine (Cassie) McMenamin, who had lost her husband John at the Somme, looked after the six children, four girls and two boys. My grandfather, Charles, was the eldest, about fifteen, going on sixteen when his father enlisted.

> Mrs. C. M'Menamin, 21, St. Columb's Wells, Derry, has been informed that her husband, Private John M'Menamin, of the Inniskillings, who was reported missing since the 1st July, is now officially notified as having been killed on that date. Mrs. M'Menamin's brother, Private Charles M'Monagle, Royal Irish Regiment (Irish Brigade), has been missing since the 3rd September, while another brother is serving with the same regiment. The soldiers were members of the Irish National Volunteers before enlisting.
>
> **A contemporary newspaper account of the death of John McMenamin also reports that Charles McMonagle is missing. John McMenamin is a great-uncle of former mayor, Pat Ramsey.**

Charles McMonagle went out with the Royal Irish Regiment and fought in the Battle of Guillemont and he was killed on 3 September 1916. His body was never found. Both John McMenamin and Charles McMonagle are listed on the Diamond War Memorial. His brother, Dennis, survived the war and he came back home to Derry. My grandfather, Charles Jnr., joined up when he was only seventeen serving in France in 1917 with the Inniskilling Fusiliers, in the Second Battalion, and was in the army until 1920 or 1921 when he came out and returned to Derry. I knew my great-grandfather had served in the First World War but never knew my grandfather had fought in the same war until after he died. My grandfather helped rear his brothers and sisters by sending back bits of money from the army. The brothers and sisters were mostly brought up in the Wells. My grandfather continued to live in 7 Joseph Street where my great-grandfather had lived and where we lived till we moved in the 1960's when the whole area was "tumbled" and re-developed.

Those wee houses were what nowadays they call dwellings of multiple occupancy. Two or three families lived in that one house where the six children had been living. There were a couple of other men who had lived there too who lost their lives in the First World War. A lot of families in that area lost relations at that time. Mostly you hear about young men going off - like my grandfather at 17, 18, but my great-grandfather was in his late thirties when he went to France and never came back. He left the eldest child in charge of the younger five - four girls and a boy. It was a lot of responsibility. Then again it was a different time. People left school at thirteen or fourteen and were out working, earning a living. There were different expectations then. Girls mostly ended up in the shirt factories. Young people took on big responsibilities.

My mother, who is still with us, remembers going to the the War Memorial in the Diamond. My grandmother McMonagle was invited and my mother went up with her. She was just a wee girl at the time. At that time as well as poppies as symbols of remembrance, people made up their own wreathes of white flowers or lilies. For a couple of years after that, seats were reserved for the families of soldiers who had died. Then the Catholic population veered away. There were lots of reasons for this. I think the symbolism put them off. I know my mother said it came to a time when she felt uncomfortable because the ceremony was very pro-British. When you think about it, the 'Britishness' was a natural thing, historically. But it was difficult for those families because of the increasing stigma around Catholics being involved in the British forces, particularly after the Easter Rising of 1916. A lot of families didn't talk about it. Like many other Catholic families in Derry and throughout Ireland, they stopped talking about it. For Republican families it became a taboo thing. For other families I don't think it was a taboo but it was something that just wasn't talked about. Still there was quite a number of people from the Catholic community who joined the British Army in the Second World War and who are only beginning to talk about it now. My own father, George Hasson, was one of those.

Because they weren't in the 36th (Ulster) Division, these men have been somewhat forgotten. It wasn't necessarily that they were airbrushed out. It was the political situation in Ireland that subsequently dictated.

I have my great-grandfather's medals - the 1914-15 Service Medal and the ribbon for the Victory Medal. I don't know what happened to the Victory Medal itself. It was in the family a long time. His name was misspelt on the back of his Service Medal, but it has his regimental number. There was also a memorial plaque given to the family. It used to be in a frame on the wall but my grandfather kept it in a cupboard along with the Death Penny. The medals were put away. When I was a wee boy we still had that picture hanging up in the kitchen of our house, of a man in uniform. It was my great-grandfather in his Royal Irish Regiment uniform.

Everyone of my grandfather's family - all the siblings - all had that picture in their house of my great-grandfather in his uniform. One of my grandfather's sisters married a staunch Republican. It was funny to go into their house because on one wall, there was a picture of Patrick Pearce and on an other wall, a picture of my great-grandfather in his British Army uniform. My grandfather's sister, Maggie Anne, married a Protestant man called Alec Platt and they lived in Lower Road. She converted to the Church Of Ireland. I used to go over to their house after school to watch their black and white TV and get sweets. She was a bit of "a tartar" but he was a lovely man. On one wall there was a picture of the Queen. On the other wall a picture of my great-grandfather in his uniform. My grandfather used to go up and he would say *"Look at that there, a picture of the queen and a picture of my father, side by side."*

When I was a child there were a lot of Catholic houses with these sort of "shrines". It just wasn't talked about outside the family. And families with very strong republican tendencies didn't want to acknowledge that there was

1 George Hasson married Ginny Lamberton on April 21st, 1919. 2 Second World War photograph dated 1942. 3 George Hasson, chimney sweep, post-war 1947.

someone in their family who had been a British soldier or wore a British uniform. There is an illusion that has been cultivated over the past generation that Derry was always a staunchly republican city. I knew people who had republican sympathies but the vast majority of people in this town didn't have this strong link. They saw themselves as nationalists with a small "n" as opposed to a big "N". People were too busy trying to make a living and bring up their weans. There were families in Creggan, in the Bogside and Brandywell who were linked to the Army, the RAF and to the Navy and they weren't bothered.

My paternal grandfather, George Hasson, was a chimney sweep. He had been in the army in the First World War and the Second World War. When he came out of the army, he worked everywhere - in government buildings, at the Courthouse, police stations, schools, Catholic schools, Protestant schools. As an ex-serviceman, his business was everywhere and he knew everybody but I cannot recall him or my grandfather McMonagle ever talking about their wartime experience. My own father fought in the Second World War. He had a million funny stories about being a soldier but he never talked about the dark days. About a year before he died, when things were quieter here, more settled down, I told him we were going on a trip. Myself and my son took him in the car to Enniskillen, to Castle Barracks to the Royal Inniskilling Fusiliers Museum. It was absolutely incredible. He wandered around and by that time, he was getting a bit stooped but he stood straight and talked to the people there. When he let them know that he was a veteran, they were very taken with him. He was one of very few veterans left. I took a picture of him standing to attention beside the Regimental Badge outside the Museum. He mentioned his army number, and they knew that it wasn't from the Inniskilling Fusiliers. He said he was from the Rifles. You mean, "*the Belfast pygmies*" they said. After 60 odd years, he had been freed up to be himself and to talk. He hadn't felt like that for a long time and most of the people he served with were gone.

I was arranging to take him to the Royal Ulster Rifles Museum in Belfast but he died shortly before that."

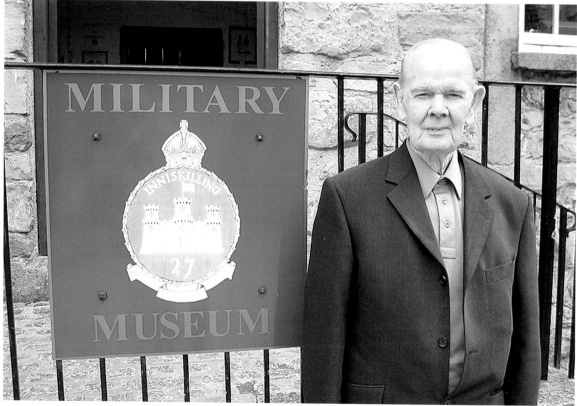

Charlie Hasson's father, George Hasson, at the Royal Inniskilling Fusiliers Military Museum, Enniskillen.

Bridget O'Toole interviews

Frank McGuinness

Bridget: Over 5,000 soldiers went from Derry to the First World War. Over a thousand of these men never came back. Was there anyone in your extended family who went to the First World War?

Frank: If there was, to be honest with you, I didn't know anything about them. I had many uncles married to my mother's sisters, who were in the Irish Army, but they didn't fight in the First World War, and they weren't there in the Second World War either. I think the father of one of these uncles died at the Battle of the Somme but I only found that out three or four years ago, so no, there is no family connection really.

Bridget: This publication '*Remembering*' has been inspired by the Diamond War Memorial in Derry. Did any such memorial inspire your play "Observe the Sons of Ulster Marching Towards the Somme"?

Enniskillen War Memorial.
(Photograph courtesy of Clive Johnston)

Frank: There were in fact two war memorials that were a spur to awaken my imagination and my feelings about the subject. One was in Enniskillen. I have a close friend from there and the memorial is in a very prominent part of the town. I actually think that the character of David Craig in my play is very much suggested by the soldier there. The other one is in Coleraine where I taught and where I had my first real eye-opener to the scale of sacrifice that was made by the Northern Irish community in the making of the First World War.

Bridget: Where did you do your research for the play?

Frank: I did my research almost entirely in Coleraine, in the Irish Library there and in the University library, and I made a lot of use of the second hand bookshops in the town which had plenty of history books going cheap at the time. The play was actually begun in Coleraine. Its whole shape was dictated by the thinking I did in Coleraine though it was finished in Dublin.

Bridget: You were in Coleraine as a lecturer in the English Department which is when I first met you. When you came to live there, did you experience any kind of culture shock arising from the fact that you grew up in Buncrana and went to university in Dublin? Did you find it very different, very surprising?

Frank: Well it was extremely different. It was the first time I had ever lived in a predominantly Protestant and Loyalist community. They have their traditions which they venerate as deeply as we venerate ours. One of those traditions is the contribution

Coleraine War Memorial. (Photograph courtesy of Jackie McColgan, Yes! Publications)

which that community has made in World War One especially, but also in World War Two. It is very much a living reality for them, not something in the history books. I think I probably would not have written the play if I had not been exposed to the enormous significance which that community places on those global events. I have no doubt about that.

Bridget: That's interesting because one of the feelings you get from the play is that sense of the continuity, the whole texture and feeling of the play is about the future and the past, even though it ends with Battle of the Somme.

Frank: Well I think the Somme was an act of improbable bravery and terrifying heroism. I think even the most biased eyes can see that. The play confirms the worth of studying another community's history. That really did become apparent to me the more I investigated it. I had never been given access to such material in my own education, either through the study of my country's literature or the island's literature if you like, nor through the study of the island's history. It was very much a censored version we had and I've always tried in my writing to take on the forces of censorship. Tackling the subject of the Ulster contribution in the First World War was very much part and parcel of that confrontation with censorship.

Bridget: Do you think the reason the First World War was not commemorated in the Nationalist community had to do with Easter 1916 and what followed?

Frank: I think it is too simplistic to say that. It is a part of the reason, but arose out of the enmity between Ireland and England, that whole suspicion of the British Army, British Empire and British police forces which persisted well beyond 1916 and went right through up to the 1990's. It was only then that the Nationalist community began to take stock of the fact that we were shaped by these events as well, and that many people from the Nationalist community went to fight too. It's just being more honest with ourselves really when we recognise that contribution. I'm all in favour of that.

Bridget: I remember being quite shocked when I first came to live here by the fact that the Catholic community didn't seem at all to observe Remembrance Sunday.

Frank: They make up for that in their remembrance of their own past deeds. When I was home in Donegal on Easter Sunday, there was a large gathering of Sinn Fein in the graveyard. It was quite strange to see it there, a political meeting happening in a graveyard. So the worship of the dead is a worship shared by both sides. It just depends on which dead you care to commemorate.

Bridget: Did those men in "Observe the Sons of Ulster" die for Ulster?

Frank: Yes ... and for each other ... they were Ulster.

The Diamond War Memorial in a bleak mid-winter.
(Photograph courtesy of the Bigger McDonald Collection).

Peter Atkinson remembers
John Mercier Atkinson and Donald McGowan

" My grandfather was a Belfast man, John Mercier Atkinson. He was twenty six when he was killed. Fatally wounded on 1 July 1916 at the battle of the Somme, going 'over the top', he died nine days later on July 10th.

John Mercier was not long married to Jeannie McGowan from up in the Fountain. They had two children - my father, Harry and his older brother, Jim. They were just babies. It must have been very hard on my granny.

John Mercier Atkinson had an older brother, James, who had previously emigrated to Canada where he joined the Hundredth Winnipegs, enlisted to the Canadian Overseas Expeditionary Force. He came back, fought and was also killed. Donald McGowan and George McGowan, my granny's brothers, also enlisted. She had four of them in the Great War, (her husband, two brothers and her brother-in-law) all at the same time, all in different units. Donald McGowan was killed at the Somme. Of the four of them, only one survived, her older brother George, who came home wounded. She also lost a nephew, George's son, in the Second World War.

I don't know very much about John Mercier's early life. He enlisted in Liverpool, into the Second Inniskillings and ended up

Donald McGowan

back here in Ebrington Barracks where he met Jeannie. They got married in Carlisle Road Presbyterian Church. His name is inscribed on the church memorial there but not on the Cenotaph. He had settled here with Jeannie, living at 55 Fountain St. His death notice shows this address. On the marriage certificate, it simply says, *"Soldier, France"*. His father was a postmaster in Belfast. That's all I can really tell you, I don't know much about them but you can tell that they must have been pretty well respected and pretty well educated. The only clue I have about why he

The Death Penny sent to the McGowan family to honour Donald McGowan killed in action at the Somme on July 1st, 1916.

Right – Donald McGowan remembered by the Murray Club of the Apprentice Boys in their Roll of Honour.

Albert McCarter, a fellow member of the Murray Club, subsequently mentioned by Wesley Maultsaid in correspondence (see page 90), was also killed at the Somme.

PARENT CLUB ROLL OF HONOUR

1914-18 WAR

MISSING—Brs. Robert Russell, William Simms, William Dunlop.

KILLED IN ACTION—Brs. James Roulstone, George Stirling, Donald McGowan, Ernest Boyd, William J. Pollock, William Mitchell, Robert Hamilton, Alexander Miller, Thomas Mills, William Hamilton, Albert McCarter, Thomas Allen, George C. Maguire, Robert Kelly.

ACTIVE SERVICE—Brs. William Finlay, John Brown, Robert Cowan, W. Ernest McCarter, Andrew White, Adam Neely, Robert Reid, Samuel Moore, Joseph Warke, Wesley Arbuckle, Joseph Burnside, Lewis Williamson, John Quigley, Robert Anderson, John Dixon, William J. Lowry, William Mooney, Charles Hamilton, Thomas Wilson, William McGarvey, Alexander McGregor, Thomas Orr, Harry Wilson, William J. McLaughlin, John Nicholl, John C. Lappin, William Logue, Andrew Adams, James Scott Whyte, William Smyth, Hamilton Mooney, Joseph Black, William Bradley, Thomas Donnell, William McCarter, William Dougherty, James S. Connor, George Gardiner, Thomas Fulton, John Hill, David Miller, Joseph Allison, James S.

Donald McGowan, on right, pictured with brothers Thomas and David McGowan (no relation) from Bond's Place. All died in the First World War.

Granny Page (nee Elliott) and George Henry Williams, side by side in the locket he gave her before he went off to war.

The death certificate for John Elliott

enlisted in Liverpool is that his mother came from Liverpool. John Mercier Atkinson signed the Ulster Covenant, in Belfast.

The war medals are what stirred my interest. Three sets of medals, two from the First World War and one from the Second World War always lay in the drawer at home and when my parents died and we were going through the house, I took the medals. These men had fought a war. Their medals were lying in a drawer and nobody knew anything about them. John Mercier Atkinson had the full set of medals, bronze, silver and gold plus the Death Penny. So had Donald. His brother George who came home wounded had the three medals. I have the medals, Death Pennies and documents. I want to get the medals mounted.

My father was a good loving man but it is sad that he grew up without knowing his father or his father's family circle. He was only a baby, just a year old in 1916. Neither my father (Harry) nor his older brother (Jim) ever talked about their loss. My father didn't talk about his own experiences in the Second World War either. When I see archive film footage of the First World War, the images are horrendous but they help me picture what it was like for my grandfather and my great-uncles.

Over the last six years I have researched all the family connections. My granny Page, on my mother's side, lost her fiancé going 'over the top' on the 1st July. Her fiancé was George Henry Williams, Company Sergeant Major of Eleventh Battalion, Royal Inniskillings. She also lost her cousin, Rifleman John Elliott, (Tenth Battalion, Royal Irish Rifles) on 22 November 1917 at Cambrai. She had a brother who returned home, Sapper Thomas Elliott of 121 Field Company Engineers.

Before George Henry Williams went off to the war, he gave my granny Page a silver locket which my cousin in Australia now has and keeps safe. The locket is a cherished family heirloom. Although

The funeral procession of John McGowan passing down Carlisle Road.

my granny lost her fiancé in the war, she then married a Private Stephen Page from the Second Royal Scots. He was a career soldier who had joined up first of all in 1901, served in India fighting against the Afghans and later served in Burma. He fought at the Battle of the Somme and at the Battle of Mons. He was given the Mons star - he was an "Old Contemptible." He was injured at the Somme and was brought back but he didn't want to come out so they put him in the Army Service Corps. He ended up here at Dunree Fort and Ebrington Barracks. He was a committed soldier, a hardy wee man, "wee Jock", they called him.

Altogether there were so many family members who served. On my granny Page's side - her sister-in-law's two brothers were McConnell. Private David George, was killed and his brother, Tommy, came home. Tommy was in 10th Inniskillings, David George was in B Company 9th Royal Inniskillings Fusiliers. Another fatality.

My granny McGowan had a brother who was a fireman here. He lost his life too. Johnny McGowan was thirty when he lost his life. So not only in the war but even at home, Jeannie was losing her brothers.

My granny lost her husband and her brother Donald in the war. Her second brother came home wounded and she lost another brother, a fireman here in the town. How did that woman cope and get on with life? She never married again. Jeannie's other brother Sandy (Alexander McGowan) went on to become a prominent councillor in the city. He was also a well known lay preacher and had a shop at 72 Fountain Street, "Granny McGowan's".

What do John Mercier Atkinson or Donald McGowan mean to me now? You have to honour them. When they went off to the war, they were too young to even have had a life. John Mercier was just a couple of years married to my granny. I suppose in those days, they joined up for a bit of money, a wage to put clothing on their back and food in their bellies. Probably for a lot of men that's what it was. Of course there was patriotism as well and when you look at all the lists of the men who joined up, everybody knew everybody. If one went, they all went. They all went together.

Postscript

Because of the Troubles I never went much to the Cenotaph to pay my respects. You would worry about who was looking or who was behind you. I always had that fear so I kept myself to myself. Now I go up and I have no problems because of the times we are living in. The gates are open and that helps and I don't care who's behind me. At the end of the day it's about remembrance of the dead. When I put that poppy on, I put it on for my family, for my great-uncles, my grandfather, for no other reason. I don't hesitate to show my emotions. There's not a Remembrance Sunday that passes but there's a tear in my eye. That's the way I am. One thing annoys me though – there are two family names of ours not on the War Memorial. John Mercier Atkinson's name isn't there nor is that of young John Elliott. John Elliott lived here, in Lewis Street, Rosemount. I'd love to go up and chisel them on myself."

Jeanette Warke remembers

James McBride

Sadly, I don't know a lot about the early life of my grandfather, James McBride. I only became aware of him when my mum used to get me to fetch the big Death Penny out of the drawer of the sideboard in the family home in Belleview Avenue for polishing. There was a name inscribed on it, "James McBride". My father was John McBride. I used to ask him *"Is this yours?"* For years he never told us that it related to his father. He always held a great silence about it.

When I started to research my grandfather's life, I discovered that he went away to fight in the First World War leaving behind a very young family. My father was eight years of age when his father was killed. He was the fourth youngest in a family of six. I was told by an uncle that, at the time the family got the tragic news, my daddy ran away from home.

My grannie Elizabeth (Lizzie) McBride was left with the six children, the three older ones, my father and two younger children. James, the eldest was born in 1902, then Mary

My father John, my mother Martha and my sister, Anne.

Elizabeth, born three years later in 1905, Henry Alexander was born in 1907. My father was born in 1908. Sarah was born in 1911 and Ernest Kitchener was born in 1914. Can you imagine what it was like, a very small house, "a door and a window" as we would say, in 17 Fountain Place. I often ask myself, *"How did Lizzie feel the day she got the letter or the knock at the door, telling her that her husband had been killed, going over the top?"*

As patriots, James McBride signed the Ulster Covenant in 1912, himself and Lizzie. I would guess too that he joined up for the money. There was no money in the home. He was thirty three when he died on the first of July 1916. I would love a photograph of my granda and my grannie. We don't have any. My father never ever told us we had aunts and uncles. He never talked about his mother. He never talked about his father who had been killed in the war. All we had was the big Death Penny, lingering in the sideboard drawer.

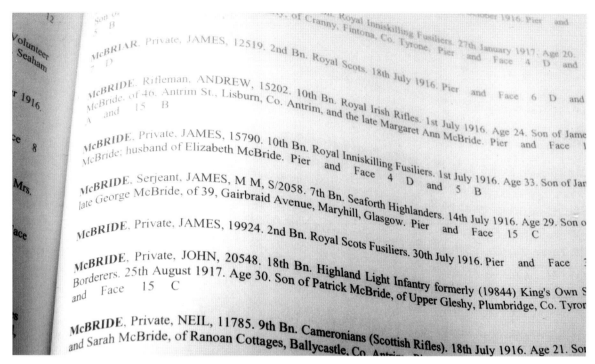

James McBride's name on the Thiepval Roll of Honour

Years later, my daddy joined up and served in the Second World War. We have photos of him in China and Cairo. I was born in 1944 and when my daddy came home, I didn't know him. They tell me I squealed because this "strange" man came into the house. I remember my father burning his medals in the range. He burnt them because they had neither jobs nor pensions for the soldiers when they came home from the War. They had nothing. He felt very let down.

When I got interested in the First World War and had the opportunity to go to the Somme in 2002, I was very full of expectation. I had thought that James Mc Bride would have a grave. People said there might not be a grave but I had it in my heart that I would find a grave. There was no grave. But my grandfather's name is on the Thiepval Memorial. I'll never forget that day, stood looking at his name and asking myself, *"What was it all about, my grandfather's name on a lump of stone, that poor man dead out here, leaving his wife and children behind, all six of them?"* He hadn't got a grave. 'He went over the top on the 1st July 1916 at 7.30 in the morning', and, as far as I know, bodies, where they could find them, weren't got out of the mud for months and months afterwards.

Now I go every year. I get a great peace out of standing there at the Ulster Tower, the Menin Gate and at Thiepval. Thiepval is the place I get the most connection - that's where they were in those trenches before they went 'over the top' that morning. I feel a great closeness there. James McBride is remembered in that his granddaughter is there.

My grandfather's death devastated the family. His wife, Lizzie, died only four years after him. I've been told by people in the Fountain – though they were very reluctant to discuss it with me - that the family was "farmed out", as they put it. Neighbours and family friends took them in. My

Jeanette Warke at her grandmother's grave in the city cemetery.

father was taken in by Granny Molloy. My father went away to serve in the Second World War with George Molloy. My daddy and George Molloy married two sisters - that's my mammy and her sister, Annie. My daddy was always very quiet and withdrawn, probably because of what he suffered growing up. Some of them went over to Cuthbert Street to the Brennans. I think two of the brothers went to Belfast because one of them, the eldest, James became a champion boxer there. Ernest died in Belfast in a home for soldiers so he too must have got involved in the Second World War as well. I have a Bible belonging to him that was sent to my mammy after his death.

I always wondered what happened to my granny? She died in 1920. What did she die of? And where were her remains? I started to hunt about and then discovered that she was most probably buried in the City Cemetery. I was up and down then to the City Cemetery but could get no information on Elizabeth McBride. Finally on the 4th January 2006, I was talking to John Taggart in the Registry Office. He suggested looking under a different name. Maybe it wasn't Elizabeth McBride. We looked under Lizzie McBride and there she was, Lizzie McBride from 17 Fountain Place. It was like winning the lotto. I can't describe how it felt. He had the number of the grave. He said there might not be a headstone.

It was getting dark when we came upon the plot. There were no markings on it, nothing at all. Obviously a lot of people were buried there. In the Registry Office at the cemetery, they were able to tell me that she died on 4th January 1920. I found her on 4th January 2006."

The Menin Gate at dusk. (Photograph courtesy of Jeanette Warke).

Norman Orr remembers

Robert Orr

Norman Orr pointing to his father's and uncle Robert's names on the North of Ireland Shipbuilding Company Roll of Honour displayed at the British Legion premises on Iona Terrace. (Photograph courtesy of Jackie McColgan, Yes! Publications)

“ My name is Norman Orr and my father, Thomas Albert Orr, served in the 1914-18 war, alongside his brother Robert. My father came home safe but Robert was killed on 1st July 1916, at the Battle of the Somme.

Robert was two years older than my father. They had joined up together on the same day in 1914 down at the Swilly Railway station on the Strand Road. They had probably stood side by side in the same queue as there is only one number's difference between my father's number and Robert's. They were both apprentice riveters in the shipyard in Londonderry. My grandfather, William (Willie) Orr, lived at the bottom of the Rock Road. The Orr's had moved in from the Culmore area. Willie was in charge of the stables in the Rock Bakery which was across the road and is now converted into apartments for the university. At that time it was all horse drawn vehicles.

My father, like all old soldiers, very seldom spoke about the war. In fact I never heard him talk about it at all. In those days, fathers didn't talk to their sons like they might do now. You were "seen but not heard." As a child, whenever I went down to old Willie's, I had to be on my best behaviour.

Thomas Orr, on right, making deliveries for the Rock Bread & Biscuit Company.

Otherwise I would have been sharply told off, or put out to the back garden to play myself while the grown-ups talked. When I was older, I didn't really approach my father about his war years. He would have thought I was asking about something private. I knew that he just didn't want to talk about it.

My aunt Gwen used to tell how, before they went away to war, Robert and my father went out to Steelstown to a tin hut where they held dances. Robert, she said, was a great dancer. All the girls wanted to dance with him. Listening to my aunt, I see Robert as one of those wild fellows who got in there and mixed with different people. Years ago, aunt Gwen showed a photo of Robert to my wife. I regret that we didn't ask for that photo because now those photos have all but disappeared.

My father was born in 1898 which made him sixteen when he joined up. Robert was born in 1896, joined up at eighteen. He was twenty years of age when he was killed. Robert was one of the first wave to go over to France and my father was coming along in the next move up. Through the years I have wondered what my father's thoughts were. He must have known that his brother had already been killed. What was it like for him to know that his brother was dead and have nobody out there at the Somme to comfort him like his father and mother would have done at home.

When my father came out of the Army after the war, he joined the 'A' Specials, moving in the early 1920's up by Newtownbutler in Fermanagh. That's where he met my mother and they were

Worshipful Master Thomas Orr holding the Bible.

married around 1923. He came through the First World War with neither scrape nor scratch but he was wounded with the Specials. They were ambushed by the IRA somewhere between Newtownbutler and Clones. I remember my aunts up there, Mary and Lizzie, saying there was no anaesthetics for operations then. A doctor from Newtownbutler got the bullet out of him by prodding and poking - '*Imagine, to come through the four years of the First World War and then get wounded back in his own country*'.

When the family moved back to Derry from Fermanagh, my father was offered a house in the newly built Messines Park but he decided to buy his own house up at Epworth Street in Rosemount. That's where I was born in 1930. We moved out to Eglinton in 1936 when my father let the house in Epworth Street to an ex-soldier, by the name of Long, who had served with him in the war. I remember his friend had lost a leg, and when he came up to us, he used to stump about on a wooden leg.

By that time my father was also working in the Rock Bakery, as a bread server. I think he won shows at the Brandywell with the horse drawn vehicles. When Willie Craig left the Rock Bakery to form the Abercorn Bakery Company up off Bishop Street, my father went with him. They were motorised by then and my father learned to drive.

At the start of the Second World War, a local councillor encouraged my father to join the

Admiralty Police. He left the bread baking business behind, joined up and got promoted to Sergeant. He remained with the Admiralty Police until he died from cancer in 1954. Possibly the First World War didn't help - he never said anything about the gas - and like everyone else in those days, he smoked. I only wish my father had said something that I would have been able to pass on. I was away in the RAF in 1950 when the family moved back to Epworth Street. My father never really did well after his return to Derry. He died four years later. He loved living out at Eglinton, out in the country. He had a lovely garden and an orchard which he never left. He kept it in great order. He grew everything - apples, goose-berries, blackcurrants, redcurrants and he had two plum trees - Victoria plums. He was fifty-six when he died, a young man.

My father was in the Apprentice Boys. He was in the Orange Order and I think he was in the Royal Black Preceptory too. I remember one big photograph in particular. He must have been Worshipful Master because he has the Bible open in front of him. I have his First World War medals. I don't wear them. I keep them framed.

Norman Orr outside the British Legion with the Death Penny commemorating his uncle, Robert Orr. (Photograph courtesy of Jackie McColgan, Yes! Publications)

Currently I am chairman of the Friends of the Somme Association here in Londonderry. I've been out a couple of times to the Somme. My father had never been back there. It was only in the eighties or nineties, we started to have those tours. We went out in the 1990's with the Somme Association accompanied by Ian Bartlett and Marlene Jefferson, the former mayor. It was actually Marlene who pointed out Robert's name to me on the Thiepval Memorial. I had written to the War Graves Commission and they had informed me where his name is inscribed because his body had never been found. I went out for a second time with the Hamilton Band who of course were the band of the Londonderry Battalion 10th Royal Inniskillings. The first time I saw Robert's name, I felt very sad. I wish I knew more about him. All I have are the few wee stories that Aunt Gwen told us about him and life on the Strand Road, years ago. I know that Robert and my father were very close, the more so since their mother had died when they were so young. My father was five and Robert seven, when she passed away in 1903.

A lot of the members in the Somme Association go to France or Belgium but you struggle to get them to come on the 1st July Parade we have here in Derry. Some come but not the numbers I would expect. I say 'Come to the 1st July, come to the Cenotaph, come to where the names of those people who fell at the Somme are remembered.' I always lay the wreath on behalf of the Somme Association although it's the Hamilton Band that organises the parade, not the Somme Association. For years and years I've been there, just to remember the dead. It's a pilgrimage. Robert was twenty and there were fellows who were only sixteen and younger. And of course in the autumn of 1914, they expected the war to be over "by Christmas."

Postscript

I am involved too with the Waterside Branch of the British Legion and eventually became its Treasurer and Vice Chairman. One night during the Troubles, Bobby Bruce, an ex-Second World War man from the Harbour Board, said to me 'There is a Roll of Honour over there in the Harbour Board and with all these bombs going off, it's going to be destroyed some night - would you take it into the Legion?' The Legion committee agreed and the first night we had it, I saw that it included my father's name and Robert's. It had come from the Londonderry Shipbuilding Company. It was in perfect order, framed and glass fronted. Here were the two names, side by side, again. I couldn't believe it."

Adam Allison Stewart, on left, with colleagues at Finner Camp.

Garry Ming remembers

Adam Allison Stewart

The young soldier Adam Stewart

"Adam Allison Stewart, only son of Sarah Jane Stewart, 21 Albert Street in the Fountain, died at the Somme on July 1st 1916. He was nineteen.

Adam was my mother's brother, my uncle. Uncle too to my sisters, Joan, Molly and Adeline, my brother Stewart and my late brother Allison.

Myself and my wife Joan had our honeymoon in France forty-six years ago. We toured around the north of France and went to Thiepval where Adam's name is engraved on the monument. It was lashing with rain. I remember it well, under the umbrella, taking photographs. Thiepval is a very emotional place. You can see it standing tall from miles away. It's a quiet place. You stand there and everyone's quiet

My parents must have had a longing to go to France but they never even had electricity. When I came back, my Aunts Mary and Ruby were still in Albert Street. They were emotional when I told them that we had been there. They couldn't understand that there wasn't a grave or what Thiepval looked like.

We always knew about Adam because my aunts always had a big photograph of him on the stairs, though when I was younger, I never really asked any questions about him.

Adam was born on 11 May 1897 in Limavady. My grandmother's husband, Thomas Stewart, died and she married another man, McMoyle. Aunt Mary and Aunt Ruby are Stewart and my mother and Adeline are McMoyle.

They moved up to Londonderry, living first at 185 Bishop Street for a while, then moved back into the Fountain, to 21 Albert Street. Adam attended Carlisle Road Public Elementary School, joined the Carlisle Road Company of the Boys Brigade and Carlisle Road Presbyterian Church was the family church. Adam is commemorated on the plaque in the church.

During an evangelical mission in 1911, when he was about fourteen, Adam accepted Christ as his Saviour and made a Christian commitment to the Lord Jesus Christ. In 1912 he signed the

Covenant (see image on right). He was also in the Murray Club of the Apprentice Boys and a member of Carson's UVF - number 1719.

In his letters, he never mentions the horrors of the war. Maybe they weren't allowed though there's nothing rubbed out in these letters. My Aunt Mary kept these things. She was the eldest, Adam came after Mary. I have his pocket companion too, bloodied and all that. His name is on it: Private Adam Allison Stewart. According to the authorities he was killed at the Somme by a shell. But his dog tag is here so how did they get that off him if he was missing? I asked that question at the Somme but nobody could answer.

My granny was seven months pregnant with Ada when they heard Adam was killed. My Aunt Ada was born on 1 September 1916. My granny had lost her only son. My mother, wee Lizzie of the letters, had lost her brother, as had my aunts, Mary and Ruby. My grandmother had a memorial scroll hanging up in Albert Street. I don't even think it was framed. They must have seen it every day.

Often on Remembrance Sunday morning when I hear of "the great sacrifice", I think of Adam. I never disagreed with the war but I feel it was a waste. I feel for my granny who worshipped her only son, the only uncle we had on that side. My granny died before I was married, about fifty years ago. I never remember dates.

Postscript

On Remembrance Sunday I just stand in silence. I don't parade. Some people wear medals belonging to their relations but I go and I simply remember Adam. I get a flag and a poppy stick and write his name, from Adeline and all the brothers and sisters and stick it in the ground. Or I let my sister Adeline do it. Keep it in the family. There's only her and me who live here now. I've been going to the Diamond on Remembrance Sunday all my life. I don't go anywhere on 1 July. I want Adam's memory to be highlighted. His name is on the War Memorial. That's special. I would like to know who died alongside him? I still think of him as the uncle we never had.

Adam Allison Stewart's signature on the Ulster Covenant (fourth from bottom)

"C" Coy.
10th R. Inn. F.
B.E.F 25/6/1916

My Dear Mother,

Just a few lines to let you know that I am well hoping this will find you all the same. I received your ever kind and welcome letter to-day glad to see by it that you are all well. I got your parcel with the buttons and I sent you an answer letting you know. G. Allen is at the Base so he can get Memorial cards and things like that but where we are you can get nothing. R. Allen is back

Adam writing to his mother in the Fountain six days before the beginning of the Battle of the Somme.

(2)

with us again and he is alright.
You needn't send me any more
parcels or anything for there is
nothing that I need. I think
this is all at present with best
love to all not forgetting wee
Lizzie and hoping to hear from
you soon

From

Your ever-loving son
Adam.

(write soon)

Tell my Aunt Maggie and family
I was asking for them, there is
a son of Hugh Baird's here with
me from Lmavady his name is
Willie and he knows you and
was asking for you

AhS.

Maggie is Emma Barr's grandmother (see interview on Page 106).

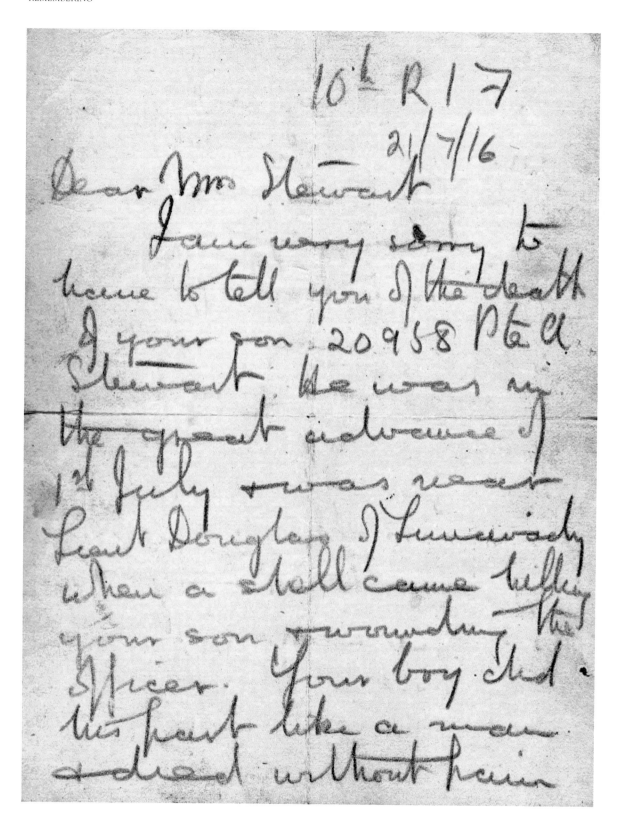

Copy of letter from Rev. J. G. Paton, Presbyterian Chaplain, at 'the Front' telling Adam's mother, Sarah Jane, of Adam's death during the "great advance" of July 1st.

which too many had to suffer. This news has only just come to hand or you would have had it sooner. You have the satisfaction of knowing that you have ~~reason to be proud of~~ your son. We all pray that you may be comforted from Above at this time.

Very sincerely yours

J.G. Paton

Presbyterian Chaplain

Fragments from the 'Pocket Companion' of Adam Allison Stewart.
(Photograph courtesy of Jackie McColgan, Yes! Publications)

Trevor Temple recalls

Rev. James Gilbert Paton, Presbyterian Chaplain

James Gilbert Paton was born in the Free Church Manse, Chapeton, Lanark, Scotland, where his father, the Reverend W. R. Paton, was minister.

He was brought up in connection with Great James Street Presbyterian congregation, Londonderry, where his grandfather, Mr A. Baxter, J.P., a former Mayor of the city, was an elder. He studied at Foyle College, and afterwards in Magee College. He graduated in 1903 from the Royal University of Ireland with honours and obtained his M.A. in 1904. He was licensed by the Derry Presbytery in 1906, and in 1907 was called unanimously to Ballykelly congregation, where he remained for four years. In 1910 he was installed in Downshire Road congregation, Newry. Three years later James was installed in Coleraine,

Rev. J. G. Paton (Photograph courtesy of Foyle and Londonderry College)

and served there for over six years. His first contact with troops was during his ministry at Coleraine, where for three months, after the outbreak of the war, he engaged in Y.M.C.A. work. His congregation loyally agreed to his request that he might be permitted to offer his services to the army and he was appointed chaplain to the forces, serving in that capacity for three-and-a-half-years with the Ulster Division. During the Great War, the Rev. Paton was a real 'soldier's padre.' One of the men wrote of him: *'He is round the firing line every night, especially if the enemy is shelling us. The boys think the world of him as the best man out here.'* Rev. Paton was awarded the Military Cross with two bars. He won the Cross in 1917 for great gallantry, and in the summer of the following year was awarded the first bar, when the London Gazette stated that: *'Under heavy shell and machine gun fire he helped to evacuate wounded, and in one instance assisted to carry a seriously wounded case four miles to an aid station. He showed fine disregard for personal safety.'* The extract quoted was published on September 16, 1918, and exactly a month later, during the attack on Mooseele his great courage brought him the second bar to his Military Cross. *'He never spared himself,'* said the Gazette. *'He worked continuously through the operations, carrying in and tending wounded, frequently passing through heavy fire to forward positions to reach the wounded. His gallant conduct and untiring efforts were admirable.'* After the war he served a further time in Coleraine before he was called to the Malone Presbyterian Church, Belfast, in 1920. He took a leading part in the scheme for the building of the Presbyterian War Memorial Hostel, in Howard Street, Belfast, and, after the opening of the hostel, served as chairman of the Hostel Committee.

His devotion to his Church had its rewards in 1931, when he was elected Moderator of the General Assembly. In that year honours were showered upon him. Queen's University conferred on him the degree of Doctor of Divinity. From the Indian Mission Church, there came a unique honour in the form of an invitation to visit India. The tour of the Indian mission stations by the Moderator was appreciated by the native churches.

James Gilbert Paton died on Saturday, February 22, 1936, after an illness of some months.

Gerard Diver remembers

John James Diver and William Diver

" My grandfather, William Diver and his older brother, my great-uncle, John James Diver, both served in the First World War. They joined up in December 1915, served in France and my great-uncle, John James Diver, was killed on August 21 1916 near Loos. His name is recorded on the War Memorial in the Diamond.

I try to imagine what my grandfather would have thought about this situation with his older brother, someone he looked up to being killed and him coming back. I think John James was in his mid twenties maybe twenty five or twenty six, a fair bit older and a man with a bit of maturity about him compared to his teenage brother. My father maintains that John James was killed in front of his brother or beside him and that William saw it happen.

My father has talked to me about his father and his uncle. Having survived the First World War, my grand-father went on to fight in the

Left to right, William Diver and John James Diver.

Second World War enlisting again in November 1939, at forty three years of age. He joined the Royal Engineers, served with the British Expeditionary Force in France up to 1940. He then served in the Middle East and finally in Crete in May 1941 when German paratroopers seized the island and captured the British soldiers stationed there. My grandfather was taken prisoner and transported to Germany where he spent four years in a prisoner-of-war camp until the Russians liberated the prisoners, probably in June 1945.

During September 2008 I went with my wife, my father and mother and my brothers to visit John James's grave in St Patrick's Cemetery at Loos. We visited the Somme and other battlefields and lots of memorials but our visit to that small cemetery was the most moving experience of our trip. By First World War standards, St Patrick's is a modest sized 'concentration cemetery', with maybe four to five hundred soldiers buried there. It was quite emotional to be there and to see John James' grave. Although I know other people who have visited, (such as a friend of mine, Seamus

ROLL OF INDIVIDUALS entitled to the Decoration granted under Army Order 20 of 1919

On Date of Disembarkation.		NAME.		Date of Dis-embarkation.	REMARKS. (a) If non-effective :—Cause, etc. (b) If transferred :—Present Regtl. No., Rank and Unit. (c) If forfeited ;—Cause.	Record of disposal of decoration. (a) Presented. (b) Despatched by Post. (c) Taken into Stock.	To l in
Regtl. No.	Rank.						
0345	Pte.	Driscoll	Augustine	2/2/15	) K.in A. 9/5/15		
10346	,,	Doyle	Edward	19/12/14	) ,, 15/3/15		
10160	L/C.	Daly	John	19/2/14	) M.A.D. 16/3/15		
25	Pte.	Devonshire	John	8/7/15	21)K.in A. 16/8/15		# authy
43	,,	Daly	John	8/7/15	21)M.A.D. 16/8/15		# authy
450	,,	Dickenson	Henry	8/7/15	21)K.in A. 8/8/15		# authy
458	,,	Doyle	Peter	17/12/15	) K.in A. 13/7/16		
701	Cpl.	Downey	Patrick	17/12/15	) ,, 9/9/16	Reld 1943 KR(912) CRV 460/Bd/3	
1885	L.C.	Dollyn	Michael	17/12/15	) ,, 6/6/16		
1986	Pte.	Daly	James	17/12/15	) D.of Wds.15/4/16		
2317	,,	Diver	John J.	17/12/15	) K.in A. 21/8/16		
2398	,,	Downey	William	17/12/15	) D.of Wds. 7/6/17	Reld 1943 KR(912) CRV 460/B d/ 3/	

I certify that according to the Official Records the individuals named in this ROLL are entitled to the Decoration as detailed above.

Official notification of the death of John James Diver, killed in action on 21st August 1916.

Gerard Diver and his father, Paddy, at the graveside of John James Diver during September, 2008.

Army Form W.3040

CONTINUATION SHEET II
CASUALTY CARD

ARMY No. 2197792   RANK SPR   SURNAME DIVER
(in block letters)

CHRISTIAN NAMES (in full) WILLIAM

UNIT..............   REGT. OR CORPS. RE

DATE OF CASUALTY	SOURCE OF INFORMATION	PRESENT LOCATION AND NATURE OF CASUALTY (to include diagnosis)	REF. No. & DATE OF A.F.W. 3016	DAT N. OF INFORM
1.6.45	W/R/D 2.6.45	LIBERATED P.O.W.	11M	5-6-
	113 Recptn Camp 5-6-45	FROM GERMANY	Q.	
		ARRIVED U.K. 1-6-45		
		ADMITTED 113 RECPTN CAMP		
		LEAVE 3-6-45 TO 19-7-45	P.O.W. 13/7	
		POSTED TO 'Y' LIST	June 45	
	C2 C3	LEAVE ADDRESS. 32 LECKY RD. LONDONDERRY N/IRELAND.	192	
	4 Aug 45		193 d/ 18 6 45	

Wt. 10521/2014 300M 5/44 T.K. & Co.Ltd./6538 51-167.

Relationship

To be completed in pencil—when required.

Name

Address of Next of Kin

William Diver was liberated on 2nd June, 1945 after four years in a German prisoner of war camp.

Breslin, whose wife, Cathy, is related to John James), I think we were probably the first people with the Diver name to have been out there. My father who is eighty one years of age now still talks about that visit. He says it was better than all the other holidays he had put together. It was so meaningful for him even though he probably didn't know an awful lot about his uncle, other than he had been killed in the First World War, until I began researching.

In the early 1920's my grandmother married my grandfather after she had lost her first husband John Rush also in the First World War. I imagine that it must have been a very common experience for young women who were widowed through the First World War to have re-married in the years afterwards.

Sometimes I ask myself what must the experience have been like for soldiers in the First World War, coming from small communities in Ireland, to be thrust into the middle of that horror. Maybe now having viewed films or dramas about the First World War, we have developed a certain degree of insight into, and knowledge about the war. However seeing a war film would be nothing like really being in a war zone and people back then would not even have had the dubious benefit of modern media. What impact did it have on soldiers to hear the continuous and thunderous roar of shellfire? Aside from the physical wounds, the constant fear of death, friends being slaughtered or dying from disease beside you - what horrendous impact must all of that have had on those soldiers who were volunteers after all? They may have enlisted with a romanticised outlook, thinking that they were embarking on a great adventure, but having no real understanding of the brutality of war that lay ahead.

This is a also a period that many Catholics and Nationalists have struggled to come to terms with.

There are so many people who served and died and to me, irrespective of what you may think about the merits of the war, these people deserve to be remembered and commemorated and their sacrifice acknowledged. Their story is part of our ancestry, part of the history of our community. I believe that it is really important that we now re-examine that history. To stand in a French village which was liberated by people from Derry during the First World War was an incredible experience. When I think about all the people who died or were injured, about those who came back and weren't acknowledged ... about those who fought in the British Army with a very clear sense of their Irishness ... From a nationalist perspective, many of the people, who were combatants in the War of Independence, got their training in the British Army and on the battlefields of Europe. We human beings with all our frailties and complexities go through different stages in our lives. We look at things differently, at different times. We think that a lot of what we are looking at is black and white, but it's actually more like shades of grey. And I wonder too what people's lives were like then – so different from ours. Our experience of poverty is minimal compared to that of people in 1914. They knew real hunger and maybe a motivation for being in the army was to earn a wage or put shoes on their feet.

I was born in 1964 and my grandfather died in 1965 when I was an infant. I would love to have chatted with him about all of this. My father has said that his father wasn't somebody who would talk about the wars too often and this seems to be a common thing with veterans. If you have been through the horrors of war, maybe you want to forget.

My grandfather was very young in the First World War. I think that officially you had to be nineteen, but I know from his Second World War papers that they corrected his date of birth, as he had falsified his age in his First World War papers to make out that he was older. I think he was about seventeen, maybe nearly eighteen when he first enlisted. Why did he volunteer to put himself through a second world war? Economic necessity might have been a big driver. If you needed the money and you had three of a family (my father and an older brother and sister, Liam and Kathleen) as he had at that stage and obviously his experience of the First World War didn't put him off. He must have thought that it was a decision worth making again. His wife, as I said, had been married to John Rush who was killed in the First World War and I think they had a couple of children. So my father had a half-brother and a half-sister as well. She had two families. I think the other children were nearly grown up at that stage because she was about eleven years older than my grandfather when they married.

My father was really fascinated to see some of his father's military records when I requested them. When he was growing up, nobody would ever have thought to get such records. People probably wouldn't have known how to go about it, so I think he is quite pleased that I have taken an interest in his family story. They help him know his father better. It's all a bit like fitting together the pieces of a jigsaw puzzle."

Joy Boyd Colhoun remembers

Victor, Henry and Thomas Thompson

Victor Logan Thompson, 8th Battalion Black Watch (Royal Highlanders) was killed in action in France on October 19th, 1916.

Henry Norman Thompson, 9th Battalion Royal Inniskillings Fusiliers, was killed in action on March 22nd, 1918.

Thomas Boyd Thompson, 1st Battalion Royal Dublin Fusiliers, drowned at sea after the Germans torpedoed the RMS Leinster on October 10th, 1918.

My name is Joy Boyd Colhoun. Boyd is a family name. My grandfather's sister, Susan Boyd, married Thomas Henry Thompson. Three of Susan and Thomas Henry Thompson's sons – Victor, Norman and Thomas perished in the First World War.

The eldest of the three boys was Norman who was killed on March 22 1918. In the 1960's, we found out that he had been engaged to a Miss Pollock, whose family owned Pollock's shoe shop on the Strand Road. An aunt of mine was friendly with Miss Pollock and occasionally went to visit her in Portstewart where she lived out her retirement. One day my aunt glimpsed a framed photograph of Norman on Miss Pollock's dressing table. She had never married. In some ways I felt sad that, in the mid 1960's, nearly fifty years after his death, she still had a photograph of Norman poised on her dressing table. Norman's brother Victor, the first of the three brothers to die, was killed in October 1916, during the First Battle of the Somme. I remember my father saying that the Thompson family had heard that Victor had been killed by a sniper. It is said too that he was last seen carrying a wounded comrade. Victor's name is recorded upon the Thiepval Memorial.

My father often used to speak about their deaths. Young Tommy Thompson, the third brother, was drowned when the RMS Leinster was torpedoed. According to my father, my grandmother, Isabel Boyd, had a terrible nightmare the night the RMS Leinster was sunk. She dreamt that she was on board a ship, that there were fierce black dogs on the ship and that they had begun to

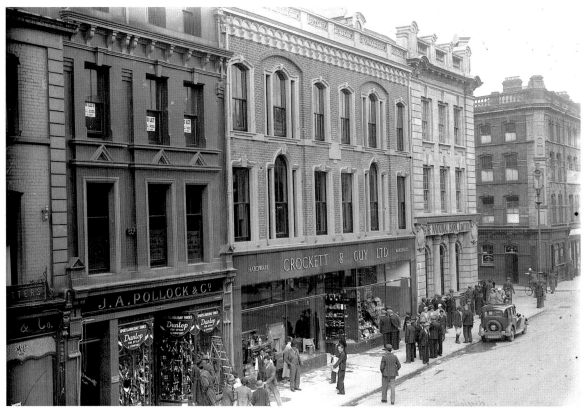

Crockett & Guy's shop was next to Pollock's on the Strand Road. Charles Love Crockett, a member of the Crockett family, died as a result of 'friendly fire' during the Easter Rising and is commemorated on the Diamond War Memorial.

Crawford Square where Winifred Thompson lived and gave music and singing lessons. (Photographs courtesy of the Bigger McDonald Collection).

devour everyone, passengers and crew. Isabel, a devout Christian, was very upset. That morning she told her family "I think something has happened to wee Tommy". They knew that he was sailing back from Kingstown/Dun Laoghaire the previous evening en route to rejoining his regiment in France. The story goes on that Mrs Thompson was out bringing in her milk at her home in Melrose Terrace when the milkman said *"That was a dreadful tragedy last night, wasn't it Mrs Thompson?"* He told her about RMS Leinster being torpedoed and she collapsed at the door. Tommy was her third son to die in that two year period from October 1916. He is buried here in the City Cemetery.

Given the colossal loss within the Thompson family, its very understandable that their father, Thomas Henry Thompson, who was a councillor with Londonderry Corporation, should become such a force within the committee given the job of creating what we now know as the Diamond War Memorial. Thomas Henry Thompson himself died suddenly after suffering a heart attack whilst attending a church service in Carlisle Road Presbyterian Church on Sunday, February 22nd, 1925. His daughter Winifred, the Church organist, was playing at that service.

I knew Winnie. My father gave me a clock, dated 1921, that Carlisle Road Presbyterian Church Choir had presented to her. My father told me that she used to be very emotional when she played the organ on November 11th.

THE IRISH TIMES.
FRIDAY, OCTOBER 11, 1918.

MAIL BOAT SUNK.

TORPEDOED BY GERMAN U-BOAT IN IRISH SEA.

HEAVY DEATH ROLL: OVER 500 VICTIMS.

SCENES DESCRIBED BY SURVIVORS.

TWENTY POSTAL OFFICIALS LOSE THEIR LIVES.

The City of Dublin mail steamer Leinster, on passage from Kingstown to Holyhead, was torpedoed and sunk yesterday by a German submarine in the Irish Channel. The vessel had its full complement of passengers, of whom a large number lost their lives.

Two torpedoes were fired, both of which took effect, and the vessel sank in a very few minutes.

The Leinster had on board 687 passengers and about 70 of a crew. The loss of life is believed to be over 500. Those lost include the captain of the Leinster, Captain Birch. It is believed that 20 of the postal staff out of 22 on board have lost their lives.

Funeral of Councillor T. H. Thompson.

The funeral of the late Councillor T. H. Thompson, Waterside, which took place to the City Cemetery on Tuesday, was attended by a very large concourse of mourners. The Corporation was represented by the Mayor and other members and officials, while the committee of the Y.M.C.A. were also in attendance, as well as the members of the Good Templar Order, the Brotherhood of St. Andrew (which Mr. Thompson founded in Derry, over two years ago), and the sessions and committee of Ebrington and Carlisle-Road Presbyterian Churches. Mr. Thompson's two daughters, Miss Winifred Thompson and Miss Muriel Thompson, accompanied the remains to the Cemetery.

The other chief mourners were – Mr. Hugh Boyd, brother-in-law, and his son, Mr. John Boyd and Miss Maggie Boyd.

Extract from the Londonderry Sentinel describing the funeral of Thomas Henry Thompson.

She was also organist in Strand Road Presbyterian Church. Winnie lived most of her life in Crawford Square after she left Melrose Terrace.

My father talked a lot about the Thompsons. He was an emotional man and got upset remembering. He worked for a food company and he used to deliver to Porter and Roulston's in

William Street. The business was owned by Muriel Thompson (Winifred's sister) and her husband. Muriel was wheelchair bound and Robbie Hamilton was in charge of the shop. One day my father was in the back store at Porter and Roulston's and saw what looked like a large coin lying on the floor. He asked *"What's that?"* and Robbie said *"That's one of those ... medal things"*. My father looked at it and he couldn't believe it. It was the Death Penny for Tommy Thompson. My father's name is Thomas Thompson Boyd. He thought it was an awful shame to see this memorial discarded in this way. Robbie said *"Take it with you - it's no good to me"* - that's how we now have it in our family.

My father really valued the Death Penny and had it cleaned up but my mother wouldn't hang it up on the wall. She gave it to me, when my father was still alive, and I remember how delighted he was when I hung it up on my wall. The Thompsons were very good to my father's family and also Winnie Thompson gave me voice training. I knew her from when I was about twelve or thirteen. I was singing in the children's choir at that stage in the church and I remember that Mrs Frame, who was the wife of the headmaster of the Model School, put myself and a couple of other girls into the Feis. I don't know who told Winnie but she met my father one day and said *"I hear you have a daughter who sings"*. He hmmm-ed and hah-ed *"Well ... you know ..."* and she said *"Send her to me and I'll tell you if she can sing or not"*. She owned a fine house in Crawford Square. The first time I went there I remember I was so frightened, when she opened the big door. She had very white hair. I was twelve or thirteen and in awe of this woman at first but grew to love her dearly. As far as I remember, I sang a verse of a hymn and she asked when could I come for lessons and that was the start of it.

Winnie never talked to me about her brothers. She must have talked to my father though because it was Winnie who gave him the photographs of the brothers that I have now. I just don't know why she never mentioned them and I never mentioned them to her. I know that the Thompsons were devout Christians and their faith would have strengthened them through their terrible loss. Maybe too there was a different attitude towards death when there was a war on. People just got on with life because there were so many deaths all round them. My father kept the photographs that Winnie Thompson gave him a long time. I have them up on my wall now.

Winnie lived alone in Crawford Square. She relied on my father quite a bit in the latter years of her life. He used to go down and do odd jobs for her. I remember one time Winnie showed me round her house. She took me into her drawing room which had beautiful furniture and antiques, all from Melrose Terrace. After she died, everything was auctioned, her jewellery - everything. She never married. She was so musical and never passed her gift on.

Postscript

My father left me a signet ring that belonged to Thomas Henry Thompson. I took it to a jeweller to see how old it was and she dated it around 1890. My father didn't wear rings himself but he used to look at this ring and say "That ring was on that man's finger when he got the word about his sons".

Eric Kirkland Beatty remembers
Wesley (Dot) Maultsaid

“ Wesley Maultsaid was my great-uncle. His father William John Maultsaid had died in 1902 and his mother Letitia died in 1908. Wesley, his younger brother Billy and his married sister Molly, who was a year or two older, lived in the family home at 11 North Street up in Rosemount. At one time the family owned 5, 7, 9 and 11 North Street. William John Maultsaid had been a successful builder in the city in the 1870's and 1880's. The houses in Clarence Avenue, West End Park and Templemore Park were all built by him.

He also built three streets up off Park Avenue in Rosemount, naming them after his sons Ernest, Wesley and his daughter Florence. At one period the family lived in Buncrana for

The young Wesley Maultsaid.

a time when William John was contracted to build the Roman Catholic chapel at Cockhill.

William John Maultsaid was originally from Rathmullan, his wife Letitia Wilson came from Derry. They were married in the Church of Ireland church at Fahan. Wesley had cousins, McGowan, from Rathmullan who also served in the First World War. Both Patrick and William McGowan were killed in action and their names are inscribed on the Church of Ireland War Memorial in Rathmullan. Two other McGowans survived. Another cousin Jim Maultsaid (known as the RIR Somme Artist) was wounded and taken prisoner but survived the war. Jim makes mention of his cousins Wesley and Billy in his war diary.

Wesley Maultsaid himself was born on 27 August 1888. He was educated at Foyle College before joining his eldest brother Ernest in the family building and contracting business following the death of his father in 1902. He then worked as a clerk in the shirt factory of A. B. Grant and Sons from 1907 to 1912 after which he moved to the Londonderry Gaslight Company. He was a keen athlete and boxer and a talented footballer. He played football for Institute in Derry and had received his first international cap in March 1914, just months before the outbreak of the First World War, when the Irish Football Association selected him to play for Ireland against Scotland.

He and his younger brother Billy had been members of the Ulster Volunteer Force and both

(MEN) *1868* SHEET No. *6*

PARLIAMENTARY DIVISION, *Derry City*

DISTRICT, _____

PLACE OF SIGNING, _____

Covenant :—

BEING CONVINCED in our consciences that Home Rule would be disastrous to the material well-being of Ulster as well as of the whole of Ireland, subversive of our civil and religious freedom, destructive of our citizenship, and perilous to the unity of the Empire, we, whose names are under-written, men of Ulster, loyal subjects of His Gracious Majesty King George V., humbly relying on the God whom our fathers in days of stress and trial confidently trusted, do hereby pledge ourselves in solemn Covenant, throughout this our time of threatened calamity, to stand by one another in defending, for ourselves and our children, our cherished position of equal citizenship in the United Kingdom, and in using all means which may be found necessary to defeat the present conspiracy to set up a Home Rule Parliament in Ireland. And in the event of such a Parliament being forced upon us, we further solemnly and mutually pledge ourselves to refuse to recognise its authority. In sure confidence that God will defend the right, we hereto subscribe our names.

And further, we individually declare that we have not already signed this Covenant.

NAME.	ADDRESS.
William Noble, Emery	11 Carlisle Road
Robert Albert Bogle	7, Princes Street
Wesley Maultsaid	1, North St, Rosemount
Robert Kerr	15 Northland Avenue
John Houston	101 Dungiven Road
Alexander Hopkins MacLaughlin	5 Carlisle Rd
Herbert Andrews	1 Barrack St
Ernest Jack	9 Spencer Road
James McCorkell	36 Carlisle Road
Jos McFahey	2 Clarence Place

Wesley Maultsaid and Alfie Bogle signed the Covenant together.

enlisted in the Royal Inniskilling Fusiliers (10th Battalion – The Derry Volunteers) in August 1914 at the beginning of the First World War. He was soon promoted to Corporal in B Company (No. 15728) and then to Sergeant. In 1916, he was transferred to the Machine Gun Company (No. 18632) but was still linked with the 10th Inniskillings. He became Company Quarter Master Sergeant before being commissioned as a 2nd Lieutenant in the Royal Irish Rifles in August 1916.

Wesley went missing on a night patrol in November 1916. His colleagues went back out to look for him. They knew he had been shot. When they couldn't find him, they believed he had been captured and taken behind the German lines. Apart from the War Office notifying the family to say that he was missing and that they knew he had been wounded, there was no other word. Eventually however the grim news came, through the Red Cross, to say he had died of his wounds. My grandmother, Norah, for a long time, believed that after the Armistice he would come back, that he was probably a prisoner-of-war. There are many such stories of mothers waiting at railway stations for sons to come home who had never been confirmed dead. Wesley was killed in action on 12th November 1916 and is buried in the Sanctuary Wood Cemetery, Ieper, West-Vlaandereren, Belgium – plot 11.J.21. He was twenty eight.

The story of Wesley's war is documented in a series of thirty nine letters (September 1914 –July

1916) that he wrote to my grandmother, Norah Kirkland, his older married sister. Norah had become something of a mother figure for the three younger Maultsaids, after the deaths of their parents. Wesley's letters stretch from when he's training at Finner Camp, subsequently at Seaford in Sussex and finally from "undisclosed" locations in France. Wesley's early letters focus as much on laundry arrangements and football matches as on training for war. Inevitably their tone darkens in the days leading up to and after July 1st 1916.

Wesley and Alfie Bogle were great friends, played football together and signed the Covenant together. Both played football for Institute and for a combined team that represented all the clubs in the North-West. I remember Wesley's international cap for his game for Ireland v Scotland being in our family home, but I don't know where it has gone to. There is a record too of the 36th (Ulster) Division having a sports day in Randalstown where he seems to have swept the board winning nearly all the events.

My grandmother talked from time to time about Wesley. She cherished his letters and other memorabilia and kept them safe for over fifty years. Wesley's official Memorial Plaque, which I still have, always sat on the windowsill at 1 Marlborough Avenue. There were always poppies in the house in November and I remember her wearing her poppy when she went out. However she would never go to church on Remembrance Sunday saying, even fifty years on, that it would be too moving for her."

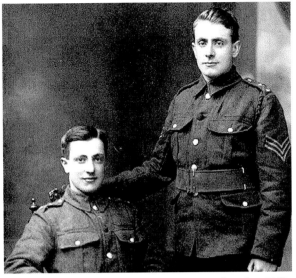

Sgt. Wesley Maultsaid and his younger brother Billy (seated). Below: Wesley's invitation to play for Ireland against Scotland.

IRISH FOOTBALL ASSOCIATION, LTD.
JUNIOR COMMITTEE.

Secretary J. Ferguson.

18 Wellington Place,

Belfast 11th March 1914.

Telephone 638.

JUNIOR INTERNATIONAL SCOTLAND V IRELAND

Dear Sir,

You have been selected to play as Centre in above match, to be played at Firhill Park, Glasgow, on 21st., March. Please let me know at once if you can play.

Yours faithfully,

Mr. Maultseed

Institute F.C.

No 15728, Cpl W Maultsaid, B Co.
10th Inniskilling Fusiliers
Finner Camp
Ballyshannon
Monday, 23rd November ,1914

Dear Norah,

Just a line to tell you I received the clothes alright. Let me know if you are making any arrangement about the washing.

Ernest says he is getting the back of Rosemount houses fixed at last. He sends me a batch of papers every week which are very acceptable.

The recruiting party were practically all country fellows except the Band. I could have got if I had asked the Sergt. Major but I didn't bother. They will be "fed-up" with the march by this time, as the weather has been rotten. Today it is snowing here and very cold, but we are warm enough in the tents with plenty of blankets. The only thing we are afraid of is the storms. Thursday night was a terror. All the big tents were carried away and some of the small ones. We are going into the huts here as soon as they are ready, but it will be a good while yet before they are ready. We are fairly comfortable except for some Chloride of Lime which was put in the water supply by the Doctor. They put in twenty times as much as he ordered and our food has been full of it ever since. It is very unpleasant I can tell you.

You might send me up a night-shirt. I think there was one in one of the batches of clothes I sent down. Bogle will be coming up on Thursday, so perhaps Maudie could give him the parcel on Wednesday night.

You must excuse the brevity of this letter as I am writing under difficulty. We will get no more leave until Xmas and then we are getting seven days. Hope you are all keeping as well as B and I are.

Yours affectionately
Wesley

Wesley, writing from Finner Camp, to his older sister, Norah, more concerned with arrangements for his washing than with the war. The 'Bogle' mentioned is Wesley's great friend, Alfie Bogle. Maudie is Wesley's girlfriend. 'B' is, of course, his brother, Billy Maultsaid.

Billy? ---- is still at the Base Depot.

Arthur in a letter recd. yesterday thinks he will join the Engineers, things are so slack with him. I have written telling him to hang on where he is if he can at all.

How about Florrie? Hope to hear good news about her soon. I am keeping in the best of health and expect soon to hear something definite about the new Machine Gun Company and my promotion. Maudie it appears is carrying on with some Officer, in Derry. Well she can please herself. I suppose she realises the truth of the old saying that a bird in the hand is worth two in the bush and is acting accordingly. At any rate it doesn't make much odds to me what she does, and I have told her in a letter to do away with the ring I gave her
....

Above: A one page fragment of a letter from Wesley, which would appear to have been written in mid to late January 1916 declaring the end of his relationship with Maude (Maudie) McLean. Up to this point, Maude appears in almost all the letters. He breaks off with her because he has learned that she is "carrying on with some Officer in Derry". There is no further reference to Maudie in any of the subsequent letters .

B.E.F.
France
17-2-16

Dear George,
Excuse the short letter but I am absolutely worked to death.

We are getting it hot here just now. Don't tell Norah, I have written her a few days ago painting things differently.

W

Wesley writing to his brother-in-law, George Kirkland, Norah's husband, telling him more of the truth from 'the Front' than he had shared with his sister, Norah.

No 2 Training Camp
A.P.O. S17
27-7-16

Dear Norah,

Sorry I could not get a chance of answering your letter sooner but after July 1st we were kept on the move constantly and I had such a lot to do that I had no chance of writing more than a P.C. I suppose you got my Field Post Cards alright and know that both Billy and I got through the first stages of the "Big Push" without hurt.

No doubt you read all about how the Division fought so I need not tell you much about what they went through. My own part in the operations was not a very heroic one. I was back with the 1st Line Transport who were comparatively safe in bivouac. We were supposed to be cut off entirely from the people in the trenches for seven days but we always managed to run the gauntlet each night with letters or additional supplies for the boys who were in the trenches. This was not, generally speaking, a dangerous job because the Germans were scarcely replying at all to the Artillery. Billy did not have to go over the "top" although he was in the trenches during the bombardment. It was very hard luck about young Albert McCarter. You can tell his people, if they don't know already, that his death was instantaneous. He was shot right through the heart. There are lots of other fellows in the Company who have fought their last fight but he is the only one you knew personally, I think. We lost 85% Officers and 83% NCOs and men, so you may guess that it was practically a new Company before I left. The drafts from the Base are nearly all Derby's Army.

I have been at the address above, for a week now. I will be here until August 9th when I go to another training centre for six weeks. The present course is only a preliminary one. The Camp is near the sea, amidst extensive sand dunes. We have had fine weather every day so far and although we are worked at top pressure from morning to night I am rather enjoying the change from the trenches. The Division or what is left of it are back in a rest area now and I don't expect they will go into the line again until made up in strength. This may take some time.

Regarding the money question I am quite agreeable to any course of action agreed upon by the others. I told Arthur, that as no one was in desperate need of the money the best thing to do was to leave it over until the November balance was struck. There may be something then worth dividing. Perhaps even, we may be Home again and The War over! Let's hope so anyhow.

Before I left the Company to come here I saw that Billy was made permanent in his present job. He will have a fairly easy time; nothing heavier to handle than a pen, and not too much of that. I am pleased to hear that you are all enjoying such good health. I'm afraid my chance of leave has gone now at least until I qualify for my Commission when I understand we all get 4 days to buy kit.

I must close now as I have some Lectures to write up. Give my love to Ethel Cooper and through her to Coopers and Cousin Tish. With fondest love to George, you and all the children.

Your affectionate brother
Wesley.
P.S. Note my new address.

Albert McCarter - Regt. No 15796 was killed 1 July 1916. The McCarter family lived at No. 5 Marlborough Avenue. Norah and George Kirkland lived at No. 1. Cousin Tish is Letitia Mooney, the schoolteacher cousin of Wesley's mother. She lived in London Street with his Aunt Elizabeth and the other members of the Cooper family.

Close family friend, 2/Lt. Robert 'Alfie' Bogle (below), writing from Fermoy, to Wesley Maultsaid's sister, Norah, on receiving news that Wesley is missing, feared dead. Alfie himself was killed at Passchendaele in August 1917.

Coy No 7
Officer Cadet Battⁿ
Moore park.
Fermoy,
Sunday

Dear Mrs Kirkland,

Have just been told Wesley is wounded and missing. I can't tell you how I feel since hearing the report as he was the only real chum I ever had.

Would you very kindly send me on any news you, have regarding him, I will be anxiously waiting a reply.

Please forgive this very forward sort of scrawl, as I hardly know what I am writing

Yours Sincerely
A Bogle. Cadet.

Right — Photograph of Wesley (back right) and three other officers he met at the 36th Division Officer Training School, France in August 1916

Below — An extract from the 'Order of Service' Unveiling and Dedication of War Memorial Window and Tablet at Christ Church, Londonderry, 30th November, 1919. Albert McCarter is also commemorated within the 'Names of the Fallen'.

Christ Church, Londonderry.

Solemn Memorial Service

(In Memory of Christ Church Men who have Fallen at the Front).

Sunday, November 30th, 1919,

At 11=30 o'clock.

MARCH FUNEBRE *(Chopin).*
HYMN 345.
SENTENCES FROM BURIAL SERVICE.
PSALMS XXIII.—XLVI.
FIRST LESSON—EZEKIEL XXXVII., to *v.* **11.**
ANTHEM—"CROSSING THE BAR" *(Barnby).*
SECOND LESSON—REVELATION VII.,
from *v.* 9.
HYMN 343 III.
CREED.
SENTENCES FROM BURIAL SERVICE
AND COLLECTS FROM
MORNING PRAYER.
HYMN 343 I.
UNVEILING AND DEDICATION OF
WAR MEMORIAL WINDOW.
HYMN 599.
SERMON BY THE LORD BISHOP.
OFFERTORY HYMN, 347.
PRAYER AND BENEDICTION.

Dead March *(Handel).*   Last Post.
National Anthem.

Christ Church, Londonderry.

NAMES OF THE FALLEN.

WILLIAM F. ALGEO, Ship's Surgeon.
HERBERT LAVEROCK, W.O., R.N.
ALEXANDER HAMILTON, Bsn., H.M.T.
JOHN KELLY, A.B., R.N.
Rev. ALEXANDER SPENCE, C.F., M.C.
Captain JOSEPH BALLINTINE.
Captain CHARLES B. WILLIAMS.
Lieutenant ERNEST M'CLURE.
Lieutenant C. G. TILLIE.
Lieutenant ERNEST WILLIAMS.
2nd Lieutenant ROBERT A. BOGLE.
2nd Lieutenant JAMES DIXON.
2nd Lieutenant VICTOR GRANSDEN.
2nd Lieutenant W. MAULTSAID.
2nd Lieutenant L. W. H. STEVENSON.
2nd Lieutenant J. ALFRED WILLIAMS.
C.S.M. GEORGE WILLIAMS.
Sergeant JAMES JACKSON, M.M.
Sergeant HUGH M'COMB.
Sergeant ALEXANDER M'INTYRE.
Sergeant JAMES ROULSTON, M.M.
Corporal JACK ADAIR.
Corporal ROBERT MARTIN.
Corporal ALBERT M'CARTER.
Lance-Corporal WILLIAM THORNTON.

[P.T.O.

Jim Arbuckle remembers
Robert Arbuckle

Robert and Tillie Arbuckle and, below, a copy of the Death Notice for Robert Arbuckle, February 1918.

" I only knew about my great-uncle Robert Arbuckle from the barest details my father had told me. His uncle Robert had served in the British Army. Then he had been a Sergeant Instructor around 1913 in the UVF because of his prior army experience. He enlisted again when the First World War erupted, served through the war, was killed and buried in Belgium. My father talked about his uncle in an affectionate sort of way. He said, *"This is a man who must be remembered for what he had done."* That was as much as I knew about him. I would have been maybe ten or eleven when I first remember my father talking about his uncle.

My daddy was born in 1908. He would have known his uncle Robert because they all lived in Ivy Terrace. My grandfather was John Arbuckle from Ivy Terrace and then Robert and William and his other brothers, my father's uncles, all lived there also. As far as I know, they all rented. They wouldn't have owned the houses. As far as I knew too, they were all from Londonderry, always had been from Londonderry, but in later years when I was looking back and trying to find out about my great-uncle Robert, it turned out that they were actually from down around Newtown-stewart, a wee place called Ballykeel, a very rural wee place. The whole family seems to have moved up to Ivy Terrace around the start of the last century, probably looking for work. It seems they were blacksmiths.

DIED OF WOUNDS.

ARBUCKLE—January 31, 1918, died of wound at C.C.S., France, Sergeant Robert Arbuckle 7789, 2nd Battalion Royal Inniskilling Fusiliers. beloved husband of Tillie Arbuckle, 34, Ivy Terrace. Deeply regretted by his sorrowing wife.

Oh, could I hear his voice once more,
And see his loving smile,
The one that would my heart still cheer.
But I must wait awhile.

A sudden change, at God's command he fell;
He had no chance to bid his friends farewell.
Affliction came, without warning given,
And bid him haste to meet his God in Heaven.
He died that we might live.

When I was looking into the whole family history, my aunt Maude, (my father's sister, her married name was Sproule) gave me lots of information and photographs. She had photographs I had never seen before and that my father never had. She had one of my great-uncle Robert in his army uniform with his Sergeant stripes posing with his wife, Tillie (Austin is her maiden name). When I look at his photograph I think, he's standing very proud in his uniform, very serious, looking directly into the camera, standing at ease with his hands behind his back. But I always look at his wife, Tillie in this photograph, and think she looks very sad, very thoughtful, almost poignant, as if she's thinking '*He's going off to war, or he's just back*'. I have no idea when the photo was taken. He was backwards and forwards. It's a poignant photograph. He doesn't display the gung-ho type, the military type "*Off to war Ho, Ho, Ho*", bearing that some old photos show. He just looks serious - proud but serious.

> * * *
>
> Mrs. Arbuckle, 34, Ivy Terrace, Derry, has received a letter from the commanding officer of the regiment stating that her husband, Sergeant Arbuckle, has died of wounds received in action. Sergeant Arbuckle, who had been three times wounded, was called up on the outbreak of war. A very popular N.C.O., he was an instructor to the U.V.F. and a member of L.O.L. 871 and the R.B.P. The many friends of the gallant sergeant will learn with deep regret of his death, and deep sympathy will go out to the widow in her great bereavement.
>
> * * *

Aunt Maude still had the cuttings of the death notice which appeared in the paper at the time. I'm not too sure which paper it was in. Aunt Maude had kept that and, I'm sure, Tillie would have kept it too.

Aunt Maude gave me the information as well about where my great-uncle was buried. Sergeant Arbuckle, 7789, buried in Dozinghem Military Cemetery in Belgium, Plot XII, Row G, Grave 11. Maude had never been there. Nobody in the family had ever been there. Nobody had ever seen that grave until I went a couple of years ago.

I went with Foyle Training Towards Reconciliation. I had heard from Tracey McRory that a trip was being organised by Glenn Barr's organisation and Sam Starrett. I got in touch with Tracey and attended a few meetings of this cross border programme. I told them at one of the meetings that I had a relative buried in Belgium and that I would like to attend his grave.

So we went out there and did all the things

Jim Arbuckle at the graveside of his great-uncle, Robert, in Dozinghem Military Cemetery.

that you had to do. Dozinghem Military Cemetery is not a big cemetery and it was easy to find. I was asked if I wanted to go myself or if the whole group could go. We all went in. We spoke to the attendant there. He looked up the records and found the headstone for us and took us down. We all stood around.

I just couldn't believe it was there, the headstone. I had a photo taken of me laying a poppy wreath that I had brought with me. I was the first from my family to visit the grave and pay *our* respects. I wrote a wee note to say that I was there on behalf of my father. I felt he would like to have been there but obviously he never was. And yet he had served in the Second World War and probably had been in Belgium but didn't take time out to go to the cemetery. For me it was an emotional experience. When I came away I was thinking it was like coming away from a funeral when you have buried a relative. All the group came around. Some people were taking photographs and then Sam Starrett said *"Do you mind if I say a few words, Jim?"* and quoted Laurence Binyon:

> *They shall not grow old, as we that are left grow old:*
>
> *Age shall not weary them, nor the years condemn.*
>
> *At the going down of the sun and in the morning We will remember them.*

I was further moved and speechless, all these things going through my head, thinking back to the war, my great-uncle Robert's grave, how he had died, how he had been found and buried when so many people hadn't been found. Then Sam said this. Then a woman who was with us from Buncrana, said a Catholic prayer over the grave. I don't remember the prayer. It was just perfect. That summed up the whole cross community feel of the trip. I'm very serious in the photo, I'm probably trying to hide my emotions. I felt tearful at the time, I really felt as if I was at a funeral, coming away from a funeral, as if I had just buried my great-uncle. I was so glad that I did it. So glad to do it for everyone, for myself but particularly for my father. As I say, I always had the feeling he would like to have gone to do that.

THE SPRIG.   83

7789 SERGEANT ROBERT ARBUCKLE,
Royal Inniskilling Fusiliers,
Died of Wounds received in action.

Joined the 1st Battalion at Londonderry in 1903, and went out in a draft to the 2nd Battalion, with whom he served in Egypt and Cyprus, being transferred to the 1st Battalion at Malta in 1908 and served there up to September, 1909, when he accompanied the 1st Battalion to North China, serving at Tient-sin and Shan-hai-kuan. He came home on the Army Reserve at the end of 1911. At the outbreak of War he rejoined the Colours at Omagh and was posted to the 2nd Battalion at Dover. Embarked for Le Havre on 22nd January on H.M.T. "Corsican." Served with the 2nd Battalion on the retirement from Mons and the advance across the Marne and the Aisne. Also was present at the fighting in Belgium from Hazebrouck, through Meteran, Bailleul, Ploegsteert, to Le Gheer, where he was severely wounded on 21st October, 1914, and invalided.

Joining the Reserve Battalion at Londonderry in January, 1915, he was employed as a Drill Instructor up till last July, when he again proceeded to join the Expeditionary Force. Shortly after rejoining his old battalion he was slightly wounded in the face, and was for a short time in hospital at the Base. He met his death a few days after rejoining from hospital.

On the right is another photograph of Sergeant Robert Arbuckle, taken from the Regimental magazine, the Sprig of Shillelagh from an edition published shortly after his death in 1918. I got this from my former teaching colleague, Gardiner Mitchell. That was when I first found out that my great-uncle Robert had been a regular soldier prior to the First World War.

'He had joined the First Battalion in Londonderry in 1903, and went out on a draft to the Second Battalion and served in Egypt, Cyprus and Malta, and he served up to 1909. Then he went to serve in North China and he came home in the Army Reserve at the end of 1911. At the outbreak of the war he rejoined the Colours at Omagh'.

Here's the Tyrone connection again - he joined up in Omagh. He was already living in Ivy Terrace and went back to Omagh to rejoin the army. Why he did that I wouldn't know.

'He served with the Second Battalion on the retirement from Mons, the advance across the Marne and the Aisne, he was fighting in Belgium from Hazebrouk through Meteran, Bailleul, from Plogsteert to Le Gheer. He was severely wounded on 21 October 1914 and invalided so he came back and joined the reserve Battalion in Londonderry in 1915; he was employed as a drill instructor and he then joined the Expeditionary Force and shortly after rejoining his old battalion he was slightly wounded in the face and he met his death a few days after rejoining from hospital'.

So he had actually been invalided out in 1914 and had rejoined again in 1915 and served right through until January 1918 when he died of his wounds.

Gardiner Mitchell said to me that my great-uncle was obviously somebody special to have his photograph in the Sprig. When we go back to the death notice that was in the paper where he was described as *"the gallant sergeant"* that sums him up for me. He was a very brave man, a military man. He liked his army service. Why else would he go back to it? Especially after being invalided out through wounds. He had served all over the world.

There is a great sense of courage and commitment to the army and a sense of patriotism, to use that old fashioned word. When war broke out, he *"rejoined the colours"*. He went off to serve 'king and country' again and again. My father always said that, prior to the war, Robert was a Sergeant Instructor in the UVF. It's in one of the death notices as well. That's the original UVF from 1913 onwards. I would assume he was in the Londonderry Battalion because he lived in Ivy Terrace at the time.

Postscript

I go to the War Memorial on Remembrance Sunday and now bring my grandsons. I go to maintain a family tradition but first of all to remember. I go to respect my great-uncle Robert's memory. I also remember my father and mother when I'm there. Both gone. So, it's not just the military thing. It's also a family thing, an act of remembrance for the whole family - aunties, uncles, grandparents and for all those I never knew for they were dead before I was born. It's all of that. There's a silence during the ceremony and that's when I think about them. Straight after we go to First Derry Church service and that's important as well. That connects the whole thing.

The War Memorial is now open and has been improved with all the flower baskets around it. It's great to see it open. It takes away the feeling that the War Memorial is something that doesn't belong to the common people of the city. In the past you couldn't get in because the gates were locked but now it's open and everyone has access to it. To my mind it's right that it's open and that everyone has access to it.

My great-uncle Robert Arbuckle's name is also recorded on a scroll and in the book of the dead in St Columb's Cathedral. He is also remembered in Ebrington Church. It's a good feeling to know that when people enlist and join up, when they have been wounded several times and then gone back, that their service and their sacrifice are remembered in these churches.

It's a good feeling to know that Robert's service and sacrifice are recognised and remembered and that people for generations to come will know that his name is there.

Some of the cast of 'Home for Christmas'. From left to right, Marcus McAuley, Ian Wallace, Nigel Norris and Mark Patterson.

Sam Starrett's grandfather, pictured centre, who was the inspiration for 'Home for Christmas'.

Richard Laird (co-writer of 'John Condon') in 'Home for Christmas'.

Roy Arbuckle reflects upon

Community arts and remembrance

Home For Christmas
(Sam Starrett)

A new play
with music
Directed by
Roy Arbuckle

'Home for Christmas' is set in
rural Drumahoe in 1916 and tells
the story of the McAuley family
both at home and in the trenches of
the Somme. The play evokes the
humour, hardship and heartbreak of
people from the Waterside in an era
which still has great resonance in
the whole of Northern Ireland.

YMCA   **8.00pm**
DRUMAHOE   **Doors**
5th-8th Nov. 1997 **open**
                7.30

FOR FURTHER INFO AND BLOCK BOOKINGS CALL: 311433
A Moveable Feast Production
(in conjunction with Londonderry YMCA, Waterside Development Trust,
Derry City Council, Arts Council NI & Cultural Traditions Group CRC)

My name is Roy Arbuckle. Roy is short for Robert. I am named after my great-uncle, Robert Arbuckle who was killed in Belgium in 1918. I also have an uncle Robert, known as Bobby, and I have a son called Robert, so we carry on the name. Robert Arbuckle was a career soldier and there has been a tradition in my family of military service which may have started with my great-uncle. During the Second World War, my father was in the British Army in the Inniskilling Fusiliers. My uncle Johnny was a career soldier too. I nearly joined up myself when I was young and broke. It was a job, and within the Protestant community, joining the army was seen as an honourable choice as well as providing an escape from high unemployment. When I was a kid, I was in the Lifeboys and then I was in the Boys' Brigade. People in the services were looked up to. It wasn't until the sixties and the American involvement in the Vietnam War, that a mass movement of people started to question the validity of war. I was probably part of the first generation of people who thought that there had to be a better way of sorting out the world than killing each other. Now when I look back at the First World War, I ask myself, *"How did the "powers that be" persuade millions of people to go to war?"* You could say that that generation was fooled. This is not a pleasant thought, not a good thing to be thinking about men who went, fought and died, gave their blood and guts, millions of them.

I am a singer-songwriter with a long-time involvement in community arts and community development. In the mid-1990's I was working with Sam Starrett and Colm Kavanagh at the Waterside Development Trust. Sam had written an original First World War story "Home for Christmas" for a Christmas edition of Fingerpost community magazine, produced by our friends at Holywell Trust. The story was "grand" but nearly forgotten until Sam let me hear some songs he'd written around the same theme: *"Flower of Ulster ... blooms of the day ... down in the fields*

... where the dead soldiers lay ...". I listened to Sam's songs and responded that I could "see" these songs being used in a play. After that we put the songs and the original story together to create the community play, "Home for Christmas".

When we worked together on the play out at the Y.M.C.A. in Drumahoe, it felt like I was opening up a well of sadness in myself that I wasn't aware of and nearly everyone who was involved in the play, whether as an actor or backstage or in the audience, said the same. I cried, especially on the opening night. Here was a story about local people, by local people, for local people in the very locality where these events had happened. It was very intimate. For the beginning of the play, I had recorded the Hamilton Band playing a medley of songs from the First World War era - *"Pack up your troubles..." "It's a long way to Tipperary."* Then the actors appeared on stage in uniform, carrying their tin hats filled with poppies. They

Imagining a world without war – Roy at the John Lennon Memorial 'Strawberry Fields', Central Park, New York.

handed one to each member of the audience and quietly said: *"Remember me"*. Everyone was moved. From that moment, people were crying. A friend of mine, Rose Gallacher, who is from Creggan came one night. She was sitting just in front of where I was working at the sound desk. At the end of the performance, she looked at me and shook her head from side to side. When I bumped into her a week later, she said she couldn't talk to me that night, she was so emotional. She said she had put the poppy amongst all her *"wee holy things"*.

Diane Greer was nervous about taking a part in the play. She said, *"I can't act."* I said *"Diane, I don't want you to act. If this war was happening now, it would be your wee fellow, Stewartie, who would be going. You're a mother, you know what that would feel like."*

The songs, all written by Sam Starrett, added something special. His song "From the Somme Back to the Foyle" is very powerful and came out of a dream Sam had about his grandfather. Five Cresswells from Sam's family went out and three were killed. His grandfather came back badly wounded. They were all from around Windmill Terrace and Hogg's Folly, all from the one wee area. To my mind, Sam's grandfather arose in his dream out of the collective unconscious of Northern Ireland.

Maybe time will heal the massive hurt of the First World War. So many families in Northern

Ireland lost somebody. They say too that there were more soldiers from the Republic killed than from Northern Ireland. We embraced our war dead more. We honoured them every year on 11th November. For a long time the same wound in the Nationalist community was little talked about. There were other priorities.

The work of Sam Starrett, Tracey McRory and Richard Laird has given a poetic voice to the Protestant community that wasn't there previously. They have offered their writing and their songs to express that collective unconscious I mentioned earlier. Their "John Condon" song is such a beautiful vehicle for the John Condon story. If they hadn't created that song, who would have known that story? Dublin singer, Frank Harte said: *"The victors write the history, the losers write the songs"* — the songs hold the memories. On the other hand, singer-songwriter, Tommy Sands said: *"The songs aren't to make you sad, they are to let the sadness go"*. People need to cry. Nature's Valium, I heard someone call it. Maybe if you aren't shedding a tear about the Cresswell family, you are frozen, you aren't as healthy as you could be. Songs can help to release that well of sadness.

The Diamond War Memorial is part of the fabric of the city and is really important to the Protestant community. Sometimes I go on Remembrance Sunday but not every year. I'm not an ex-serviceman so I don't have that bond with people who actually were in the services. They are a strong community. They have a bond there and they do their ritual. It's militaristic and it's not the way I want to remember someone. I always observe the silence at home at 11 o'clock.

And sometimes I think ... They went off there, they fought and they died - what for?"

John Condon

Copyright: Songshed
Publisher: Bardis Music

Laird / Starrett / McRory

Voice

Just a day_____ a no ther day,_____ be neath_____ the Bel gian

sun,_____ past grave on_____ grave row up on row,_____ un til I see the name_____ John

Con don. Carved in_____ stone with harp and crown,_____ lit tle cros ses in the ground,_____

_____ and stan ding_____ there my sil ent_____ prayer, is for a boy_____ who died_____ a

Chorus

sol dier. Wee lad who'll not grow old. He roes that don't come

____ home, here they_____ lie in Bel gian_____ fields and_____ Pic ar dy._____

VERSE 2

Just a recruit, in soldier's boots, from
Ireland's shores to here
this living hell, this Poelkappele, where
young men fell...
like you, John Condon ...
and all around, the harp and crown, the
crosses in the ground
stand up in proof, the bitter truth, the waste
of youth! ... that lies forgotten

CHORUS

VERSE 3

Now tell me John!... before I go on, what did
you come here for
with Ireland's bold, your life untold!
fourteen years old!
to die a soldier?
and all around, the harp and crown, the
crosses in the ground
what cause was served...?
so undeserved!

CHORUS

George and Emma Barr remember

James Hamilton Barr and Robert Finlay

George Barr

" My name is George Barr. My knowledge of my uncle, Lt. James Hamilton Barr was passed down to me through the family. My Granny Barr's house was in Aubrey Street in the Fountain. She was widowed in February 1938 when her husband William died after a long illness. I remember as a youngster of five or six, in the early forties, going up to Aubrey Street and in the wee hallway there was what we used to call the 'big penny', it seemed massive - the Death Penny. I also remember she had a framed picture of James Hamilton Barr in the hall. She had too the usual "Regret the death of" Memorial Scroll sent out at that time.

Lieutenant James Hamilton Barr

As a child I didn't really know the significance of it. We found a lot of old prizes James Barr had won at Foyle College for classical Greek and Latin. I remember big volumes of books, all very intellectual stuff. They probably eventually all disappeared. He was an outstanding student at Foyle and then won a scholarship to Queen's. The Barr's were ordinary working class people. For James to go to grammar school and then to go on to Queen's, in those days, back in the early 1900's, was quite something. He seems to have been a natural scholar.

I was older before I started to take an interest. Young people don't have the same interest in what happened in the past. James was my father's brother. My father didn't talk an awful lot about his brother but I picked up bits and pieces. He signed up at Clandeboye, was wounded in France and came home to convalesce. He then undertook light duties at the Curragh but couldn't get back out to the war quick enough. Patriotism in those days was unbelievable.

I've seen letters he wrote from 'the Front'. They're nearly all lost now. I'm sorry we never kept them. I remember in one he said that the King and the Prince of Wales had come, in a large car, to inspect them. They were lined up and James wrote, even though they had all been very dirty and muddy, it was amazing how spick and span they became, literally overnight, because they were having a visit from the King and the Prince of Wales. They formed up in some field. He said the King looked quite small, as he had visualised him being much bigger. In another letter he wrote *'that nothing exciting happening over the last few days, just a lot of rain; thank goodness the Sentinel has turned up today for there's nothing to read'*. The arrival of the Sentinel was, I suppose, the highlight of their week.

My Granny Barr passed away in 1956. Most of the memorabilia has all gone, the books, the medals, all disappeared. There is one medal in the house somewhere, maybe the Death Penny? The more time passes, the more interesting the story becomes. You're more likely to sit down and think things through, think back.

Lieutenant James Hamilton Barr was killed by a sniper's bullet at Neuve Eglise, Belgium, close to Messines. serving with the Royal Irish Rifles on the 1st of September 1918. He is commemorated on the Diamond War Memorial, in Carlisle Road Presbyterian Church, in Foyle College and at Queen's University. He was also named on the Roll of Honour at the former Presbyterian Working Men's Institute in the Diamond.

On leaving Foyle College, he had won the Irish Society's leaving scholarship of £120. The Governors of Foyle College and the Academic Council of Queen's reserved the scholarship until Lieutenant Barr was released from military service for he had gone straight to war from Queen's at eighteen years of age. Granny Barr organised with the school and the Irish Society to put the outstanding monies in a trust, creating the James Hamilton Barr Scholarship Prize for a classics scholar.

On Thursday, December 19, 1918, the headmaster of Foyle, Mr R. F. Dill, MA, paid the following glowing tribute to James Hamilton Barr: 'Most of those who are here present do not need to be told that James Barr was one of the most brilliant pupils who passed through this school in recent years. It would be impossible to give in detail all his achievements. Suffice it to say that in one memorable year, 1913, he carried off the medal for both Latin and Greek. He became editor of the school magazine in 1914, and brought it up to a high standard of merit. He left us carrying with him the Irish Society's Leaving Scholarship to Belfast University, where he gained a scholarship at entrance. Immediately afterwards he volunteered for the Army, and in due course gained his commission in the Royal Irish Rifles. When he entered the Army he had only drawn one year of the Irish Society's Scholarship, and it was suggested by his mother, Mrs William Barr, of 9, Aubrey Street, that the Irish Society should be petitioned to allow the amount of the three outstanding instalments, a sum of £90, to be devoted to the founding of a memorial prize in classics. The Irish Society has graciously assented to this proposal. Our gratitude should go out not only to the Irish Society for their great generosity, but also to Mrs Barr for making a suggestion which, if I knew James Barr, might have come straight from the true and loyal heart of her son.'

Foyle and Londonderry College continue to award the James Hamilton Barr Prize for academic excellence.

Emma and George Barr pictured by the Roll of Honour in Carlisle Road Presbyterian Church.
(Photograph courtesy of Jackie McColgan, Yes! Publications)

Granny Barr was a clever woman. She was self-taught. She learned to read from the Bible. It was her learning tool. She was said to have been a governess for the Knox's at Prehen House. We knew she had a small German Bible. I heard that she went out to Germany with the Knox's at some time or other. We found a photograph of Granny Barr and think it was actually taken in Germany with the Knox's. My father, William Barr, worked for the Derry Standard in Shipquay Street as did his father, William, before him.

Granny Barr never spoke about the death of her son. She lost James, and then a second son, Robert, died at eighteen from pleurisy. Then their daughter Henrietta died in January 1923, we think from TB. The only surviving child was my father. My mother told me a story about Henrietta. She said that just after James was killed, Henrietta was seen wearing a bright scarf. In those days, when a person went into mourning, they wore black. Somebody tackled her: *'That scarf you're wearing is far too bright.'* Henrietta replied, *'I'm not mourning with my scarf, I'm mourning with my heart.'* I'll always remember that.

Myself and my wife, Emma, belong to Carlisle Road Presbyterian Church. There are two memorials at the front of the church. On the left side, there is the memorial for the First World War and on the right side that for the Second World War. When I'm sitting at the front of the church sometimes the sun catches the brass and I can see the name Barr on it. It brings it back to me, '*That's my uncle's name up there.*'

My granda William Barr was a great churchman there. He served for many years as a Sabbath School teacher and elder at Carlisle Road Presbyterian Church."

Emma Barr

"My married name is Emma Barr. My maiden name was Emma Finlay. My uncle, Robert Finlay, died on the same day as James Hamilton Barr, September 1, 1918, fighting with the Australian Imperial Forces at Mont St. Quentin. I don't have memories or memorabilia within the family home. I didn't really know anything about Robert. I never ever remember my father talking about him. I know Robert attended the Cathedral School, the school on the left as you enter St. Columb's Cathedral.

Emma Barr's grandfather, Robert Finlay (father of Robert Jnr.), in bowler hat, at a Remembrance Day Service in the Diamond during the 1930's.

The Finlay family came originally from around Lisfannon, near Buncrana. Work would have brought them in this direction. They first moved up the Fountain, to Victoria Street and from there they moved to Linenhall Street. My grandfather later went to live with a daughter in Benvarden Avenue, in the Waterside. I grew up in Abercorn Road, opposite the parochial house. I was born there, raised there and got married from there. I was married in Carlisle Road Presbyterian Church, the family church.

My grandfather had six of a family. Robert was the third. Robert went into the tailoring business with a firm called Thompson's in Ferryquay Street where he worked for three or four years. He then took a notion that he wanted to emigrate to Australia. When the war came, he joined with the Australian Forces enlisting at Geelong West, Victoria, Australia. He was killed in action aged twenty-three. I knew Robert had been killed on 1 September 1918 but I didn't realise the significance of this until Trevor Temple was able to point out that Robert Finlay had been killed on the very same day as James Hamilton Barr. I was shocked and very emotional. When I look back I wonder why my father never told me about Robert? Why did he not talk about it? Did he join up in the Second World War because Robert had lost his life in the First World War? I don't know if there is any connection there at all.

Robert's remains are interred in Hem Farm Military Cemetery, Hem-Monacu, Somme, France. He is commemorated in St. Columb's Cathedral because he was a member of that congregation.

Knowing that we had two uncles killed on the same day has brought me and George closer together as a couple. The same tragedy has happened to both families. We are married now forty-nine years.

Postscript

Before the gates of the Diamond War Memorial were opened on a permanent basis, we felt locked out. We couldn't go in and pay homage the way we would have liked to. It was lovely when they were opened. Emma and I both go to the annual Remembrance Day Commemoration in November. We always feel sad even though we didn't know James or Robert. Their deaths were such a waste. Some brilliant people were destroyed in the First World War. James Barr was one of them. Our daughter, Gillian, has become interested in researching the family history, and is very caught up in the Barr side, because of James. There is a physical resemblance between Gillian and her great-uncle, James Hamilton Barr. Gillian is a teacher in Bridport, Dorset. Last year she took a year out to do her M.A. at Queen's in creative writing. She went to Queen's ninety years after the death of her great-uncle, James Hamilton Barr, who is commemorated on the Great War Memorial there."

Above: Waterloo Place with the Golden Teapot in the background. (Photograph courtesy of the Bigger McDonald Collection). Below: Bridge Street at the turn of the 20th century.

Terry Doherty remembers

Denis Doherty
and Robert Martin

Denis Doherty and his wife, Elizabeth.

My grandfather, Denis Doherty, who died from his wounds on November 11th 1918, the last day of the First World War, was born and reared in one of the townlands around Clonmany in County Donegal. His mother and father died from some kind of fever. Denis, and his sister, Sarah, then came to live in Derry. My great-grandfather had a sister, Hannah, living in Abbey Street and they came up and stayed with her. When Denis got married, he continued to live in Abbey Street for a year or two. Then himself and his wife moved to 51 Bridge Street. My granny Doherty was from Strabane but some of her family were already living in Bridge Street. Her maiden name was Elizabeth - Lizzie - Martin.

Bridge Street had the name of being a Republican street. Yet I would say that in that street, there were more people in the British forces than in any other street in Derry. When I recall Bridge Street, I see men in Army uniforms, men in Navy uniforms and accepted as such.

I got to know about my grandfather, Denis Doherty, from listening to my own father talking. My grandfather worked in McCullagh's, the Golden Teapot in Waterloo Place. McCullagh's were import-export people. He drove a horse and cart for them and had a button for coming in and out of the docks. As far as I know, he enlisted at the beginning of the First World War, and I think at

MEMORIAL REGISTER.

The whole of this Form should be filled up to the RIGHT OF CENTRAL LINE
and returned as early as possible to the address printed on the back.

PLEASE WRITE CLEARLY.

Surname	*Denis*	Doherty
Rank	*L Cpl*	L/ Cpl
Christian or Forenames (in full)	*Denis*	~~Daniel~~
Regimental Number	*12972*	12972
Military Honours		
Particulars of Company, Battery, etc., and, in case of Naval Units, the name of the Ship should be given		
Regiment	*6th Batt*	Royal Innis Fus,
Nature of death (if desired and if particulars are available)	*Died of Wounds 1918*	Died of Wounds
Date of death	*11th November*	11th November, 1918,
Native place of deceased (if not a native of Londonderry state connection with City)		*Native of Londonderry*
Any other particulars in reference to Soldier (if desired)		

PLEASE WRITE CLEARLY.

(Signed) *Elizabeth Doherty*   Relationship *Wife*

Address *51 Bridge st*

Londonderry

w2266

one time he actually got back home on leave and then returned to the front. My own father, Paddy, was born in 1913. Altogether Denis and Lizzie had three children - Annie, Paddy and Denis.

Given that there was no conscription, I have often wondered why my grandfather, a man from Clonmany, joined up to fight in the First World War. I remember my granny saying that her husband was a Redmondite. Recently I was approached by a man who said he recognised me because his family also originated from Bridge Street. It turned out that this man's grandfather had also joined up during the First World War, but he had survived. The man's grandfather was also a Redmondite.

I remember that there were medals belonging to my grandfather. My father reckoned he saw a picture of him as a Sergeant, but the picture that I saw showed him as a Lance-Corporal. I reckon he got "busted" for some skulduggery.

My father was five years old when his father died so he had no actual recollection of him whatsoever. He would have been three years old when he last saw his father but he would have heard stories about him from his mother, Lizzie. I was reared before the advent of television and one of the most pleasant memories I have is of my father talking about his childhood, what it was like living in Bridge Street, the characters on the street and the happenings there.

One of the things that my father remembered was his mother insisting that my grandfather be called Denis – pronounced 'Dinis' – and that his name be spelt with one 'n' and not two.

One of the most poignant images for me is that of my granny getting word soon after Armistice Day that her husband had died. She would already have known that the war was over when she received a letter or a telegram to tell her that "Dinis" was dead. And then her own brother, Robert Martin, who had also served in the First World War, died from Spanish flu on 25th January 1919. Robert's name didn't get put on the Diamond War Memorial, because he had died after the cut-off date. Robert Martin has been practically forgotten about. He's not on the War Memorial. I began to wonder did he exist at all? So I always tell people about Robert.

One of the stories that I remember my father telling me was that when the family got word that Robert was dying, my great-grandfather Martin set off to go to France. He was a tailor. Then it would have taken a lot of money to go to France, so he must have had a few pounds about him. I don't know how but he got word en route to turn back because Robert had died.

My granny's mother had died the year before, in November 1917. So within a period of roughly fourteen months, she lost her husband, her mother and her brother.

Lizzie had to be strong. She had to make all the decisions. I grew up in Alexandra Place. We went over every week to visit my granny and, if we ever went to the pictures – to the Rialto or to the Hall – we called in on the way back and got a cup of tea and a piece of bread and jam. She still lived in Bridge Street then with her brother, Johnny Martin, living next door. On Christmas Day and Boxing Day, she always came to our house, where we had 'sing-songs.' She didn't sing but I remember one Boxing Day, I saw her coming down the stairs, twirling her hair and singing *"Pack up your troubles in your old kit bag"* - that's the only time I heard her singing.

My father never really talked about his loss and he never got to Busigny in France to visit his father's grave. To my parents, who struggled to make a living, France was the other end of the world. I was the first of the family to go to my grandfather's grave. I used to go over to France camping and once I drove down to Busigny to visit the graveyard. It's well looked after. I was in my early thirties at the time. I was very emotional, more so than I had imagined, especially when I thought about how much my father would have loved to have visited the grave. I brought photos back and gave them to my Uncle Denis. Both my father and my granny had died by this time.

We always commemorated my grandfather. We always knew that his name was recorded on the Diamond War Memorial. It was no secret my family had army connections. Two of my father's cousins, who were orphans, went into the army and the air force. On Armistice Day, my family are aware that it's my grandfather's anniversary. We don't have a special Mass. My family isn't demonstrative like that. My granny was proud to have her husband's name on the War Memorial and yet she was secretive about his birthplace. When they were gathering names for the War Memorial, she was sent out a form to fill in. She wrote: *"Native of Londonderry"* even though he was born in Clonmany, and had lived there until he was eighteen years of age. With partition happening, she was taking no chances about his war pension. She had three of a family and struggled to make ends meet though she managed with the help of my great-grandfather Martin, the tailor. There's a family story that she once went to the British Legion to ask for any financial assistance she could get. An official asked her why she wasn't wearing a poppy. That offended her. She replied that she didn't need a poppy to remember her husband. She walked away and never went back. That probably soured things for the family. For that reason our family doesn't wear poppies.

My granny kept a big framed picture of Denis in his uniform hung up in the bedroom. After she died, I brought the picture to my home. When the glass got broken, I took the picture out. Behind the glass the picture was perfectly preserved, but once it was taken out, it became warped and the cardboard corrupted. I regretted that I had taken the picture out of the frame.

In recent years I have been up a couple of times to the Diamond on Remembrance Sunday. One of my difficulties there is I don't support the war in Iraq. I can pray for anybody who is killed - they have gone to meet their maker but I'm opposed to the war in Iraq. The Remembrance Ceremony gets further convoluted when they bring in all the other soldiers who have been killed here during the Troubles, and they bring in the RUC. It becomes political. The First World War wasn't political to me. When I'm standing there and they play the English National Anthem, more associated with Protestants and Britishness, I don't know how to be, where to put my hands, down by my sides or behind my back or fold my arms or ... I choose to stand with my hands behind my back. I want to be careful that I don't offend anybody by doing something wrong. I don't want to stand out and I want to be respectful. That's important. When I'm there, I'm remembering my grandfather and his colleagues. At the end of the day, he had his colleagues out there too. I'm there for them and that's also important.

Postscript

In the 1950's, my father, Paddy, used to organise bus runs around Donegal. During one of these trips, the bus stopped off at Moville. My granny used to stand her round so she went up to the bar to get my mother and father a drink. There was a man sitting at the bar and they fell into conversation, the man asking her where she was from and how she was doing. She told him of course that she was from Bridge Street in Derry. The man informed her that he had soldiered with "a man" from Bridge Street. When she asked the name, he said "Denis Doherty". He went on to tell her about being in hospital when Denis was dying. He told her everything she had wanted to know about his death, something she had longed to know all her life. The man was sat up at the bar but he couldn't move off the seat without help. He was disabled. "Look at me," he said. "Which of us has come off the worst?" The man wasn't on the bus run. He just happened to be there in Moville, in that bar, at that time. It turned out that he lived around the corner in Ivy Terrace. He was there all the time but we never knew."

Who Will You Follow?

The Men Who Fought for You in Dublin

DURING EASTER WEEK,

Or. the men who would have you sent to MEET GERMAN GUNS:

John E Redmond, M.P.,   Thos F Smyth, M.P.
F E Meehan, M.P.,   Joseph Devlin, M.P.,
T O'Donnell, M.P., and Thirty other M.P.'s **who stumped the Country TO GET RECRUITS FOR the BRITISH ARMY.**

When they appeal for your Votes Ask them when and why they stopped Recruiting.

Issued for the Limerick Sinn Fein Committee and printed at the
City Printing Co., Rutland st., Limerick.

'Who will you follow?' — This poster was published in June 1917 at a time when the levels of enlistment had fallen very low and the political tide was turning away from Redmond in favour of Sinn Fein.

Shaun and Síle Austin remember

Augustus Austin

" I was about ten or eleven, when I first heard about my grandfather, Augustus Austin, being shot dead in the Waterside in 1920. I am certain that I heard the story from my mother because my parents had split up just before I was born and after that I had no contact with my father. A friend of mine from Great James Street, Don McCafferty, told me the story too, about how my grandfather had been shot and about how the man who killed him ended up in the asylum. He was said to have run across the Craigavon Bridge, naked, shouting *"I didn't mean to kill you, Gus"* showing a great remorse which had twisted into insanity. I don't remember any dramatic moment of disclosure. It was just family knowledge that this had happened.

Augustus Austin was my father's father. My mother's father, John 'Corney' Doherty, was a Republican. He was well known for smuggling

Augustus Austin

guns for the IRA around the time of the Rising in 1916, guns which were shipped in through Derry Port. An article about this appeared in the Derry Journal some years ago - "Derry's role in the War of Independence". I grew up with stories about my maternal grandfather being seized by the Black and Tans and forced up against a wall and threatened with being shot. This happened at the top of William Street, at Lower Road, near the current site of the City Baths. My grandfather ran stables and a taxi business from there. He had the first Ford cars in Derry.

Augustus Austin lived in Gateshead, near Newcastle-upon-Tyne, but he was born in Scotland which explains how he came to enlist in the Royal Scots Fusiliers. It's not clear where in Scotland he was born. It's still a mystery how he met my grandmother. He obviously met up with her well before the outbreak of war as my father was born in July 1914. Augustus Austin joined up in August 1914. It is unclear if he was actually living here before the war or if his wife had moved back here after living over in Gateshead.

The inscription on the Austin family headstone reads:

Jesus Crucified for Sinners
have Mercy on the Soul of
AUGUSTUS AUSTIN
WHO DIED FOR HIS FAITH
24th June, 1920. Aged 27 Years.
His dear wife SARAH died 12th July 1968.
Their infant son MICHAEL died 7th Jan
1922.
R.I.P.
Erected by his wife SARAH AUSTIN

Below: The North West Echo article written by Trevor Temple.

Political Murder in Derry

By Trevor Temple

Twenty-eight year old, Augustus Austin, an ex-soldier and convert to Roman Catholicism, residing at Cross Street, Waterside, was shot and fatally injured on the evening of Thursday, June 24, 1920.

He was just turning the corner of the street when he received the mortal wound. He was conveyed to a house, and died within half-an-hour. He left a wife and family of three children. It was stated that no one could be seen in the vicinity at the time he was shot.

Austin was a native of Newcastle-on-Tyne, and was formerly in the Royal Scots Fusiliers. Since his discharge from the army he was employed by Messrs. McKeown, boot manufacturers, William Street.

He had resided in Bond Street, in a house belonging to a Protestant family, but was forced to flee from that residence, when the owner of the property received a letter warning him to clear out the 'turncoat' (the letter was addressed from Fountain Street, and was surmounted by a rough drawing of a coffin), and the house was attacked by an angry crowd. He and his family then took refuge in the house of a John Muldern.

On the night of Thursday, June 24, 1920, the supply of household coal ran out, and there was no fuel available for cooking. After seven o'clock Austin, and his brother-in-law, ventured out to secure some supplies. When Austin turned the corner of Union Street he was shot by a sniper. Friends secured the body and took it inside.

Austin's wife, interviewed, said: 'They may have wounded his body, but his soul is safe and he died a martyr for his religion.' She added 'He is one of the men they started the war over, and now that they have murdered him they should be satisfied. He was confirmed at the last Confirmation, and was a frequent Communicant. When attending the Retreat in St Columb's Church he was jeered at by gangs of Unionists. He went out to fight for them and came back to be killed by them. They have left me a widow with three children destitute on the world.'

On Tuesday, July 6, 1920, in the Police Court Mr J.P. Thompson, J.P., deputy coroner, held an inquest into the death of Augustus Austin.

Mrs Austin, the deceased's widow, said at 7 p.m. on the evening of 24th June she heard a shot and ran to the door, and said 'That is a deadly shot; some one belonging to me has been killed.'

When she reached the door her husband's body was being pulled into the house of Mrs Murphy, 15, Union Street. Mrs Austin ran to that house and saw her husband lying on the floor. She said 'Speak to me; are you dying,' but got no reply. Her husband lived, for half an hour, during which time he was unconscious. Mrs Austin left the house at 6.15 that evening.

Head Constable O'Donohue asked where the shot came from.

Mrs Austin replied from the foot of Bond Street.

The Coroner asked how she knew where the shot came from when she was in the house.

Mrs Austin replied judging by the sound that is where it came from.

Replying to a juror, Mrs Austin said there had been firing between two and four o'clock, but then it ceased until the time her husband was killed.

Joseph McGinley, 18, Cross Street, Waterside, said he saw Austin at 7.15 walking down Cross Street towards his own house. There was a shot and Austin fell. McGinley ran over, and, aided by a man named William Quinn, carried the body to a Mrs Murphy's.

Head Constable O'Donohue asked from what direction was the shot fired.

McGinley replied from Blair's Corner, at the foot of Bond Street. McGinley found the rifle bullet which killed Austin at the spot where he fell.

The bullet (produced) was a service one.

Mrs Bella Mulhern, 22, Cross Street, stated that on the evening in question she heard that Mr Austin was shot, and went to Mrs Murphy's. Mulhern heard a shot, and had previously seen a man standing at the corner of Bond Street. He waved a crowd at Blair's corner back with his hand. She did not see this man do anything else. He had something in his hand, but she could not say what it was. She could identify him. He wore grey pants.

A Dr Malseed said Austin had a gunshot wound in the chest, which penetrated the heart. This, in his opinion, was the cause of death.

The jury returned a verdict of murder, and expressed their sympathy with Austin's wife.

Mrs Austin said the trouble started in Bond's Street over her husband, and not at the Midland Station, as stated at a meeting of the Corporation. 'They sniped at my husband from Bond's Street,' she added, 'until they got him.'

Augustus Austin was wounded three times during the war. He became a Lance Corporal and transferred from the Royal Scots to the West Riding Regiment. I have his medal record from the National Archives.

When the war ended, he worked in the Labour Corps until 1920 helping to rebuild Europe after the devastation of war. He came to live in Derry in 1920. By then there were three young children, my father, my father's sister Maisie (she subsequently lived in England most of her life) and a younger brother, Michael, who died in infancy in 1922.

After my grandfather was killed, his wife Sarah (Sally) Gallagher who was originally from the Foyle Road area moved back there to live beside her mother in Alexandra Place. Augustus Austin was only twenty-seven when he was shot and at that point my grandmother was twenty-four as far as I know. Within the space of a couple of years she lost her husband and her baby, Michael, who died from pneumonia. My sister was called after my granny which is a bit strange to think about. The former mayor, Mary Bradley, grew up in Alexandra Place next door or across the road from the Austins. She told my sister that after my grandfather had been murdered, there was little or no help from the state. There was no war pension for her because my grandfather had survived the war. She did, however, receive £700 compensation. Sally was a very talented dressmaker and she used to do that intricate work of making First Communion dresses and wedding dresses. My sister told me that my father remembered as a young boy, lying in bed at night hearing the sewing machine rattling until all hours of the morning. She made a living as a dress maker.

Sally died on 12th July, 1968, but, because my mother and father had split up before I was born, I didn't get to know her.

Sarah Austin, Cross-street, was allowed £700 in respect of the death of her husband, Augustus Austin, who was shot at the corner of Cross-street on the evening of 24th June. £300 of the award was allocated equally between the three children of the deceased.

A clipping from the Londonderry Sentinel, February 12th, 1921.

Contact with my father's side of the family was not allowed, not encouraged. Other people talk about their grannies and value that sense of connection. I was only a child at the time and could have no contact with my one grandparent who was still alive.

My father too was a stranger to me. The only one time I met him was in 1989. My sister Síle was the only sibling to have had any contact with him while growing up. She was seven or eight when our parents split up. My older brother was about two. They split up a couple of months before I was born. I lost my father. He didn't die but I lost him before I was born. I speculate that the way he was brought up without his own father may have affected him and his relationships. He was the oldest, about six years of age, when his father was murdered.

When I first read Trevor Temple's story by chance in the North West Echo (on previous page) I was surprised. Even though I was aware of the story, the details I had about what actually happened were sketchy. The article was a revelation. The young family had been driven out from their home in Bond Street. Confronted with his murder, his wife Sally was quoted as saying "*They may have wounded his body but his soul is safe and he died a martyr for his religion*". I don't know what to make of that. Was she a very religious woman? I never knew her. She died when I was eleven years old. My grandfather was taking instruction at St Columb's Church on Chapel Road in order to become a Catholic. He may have already become a Catholic by the time he was shot. It may have been my grandmother who persuaded him to become a Catholic.

My father was named after his father, Kenneth Augustus. It seems to be a family tradition. My older brother is also called Kenneth. My father was a great musician. Internationally known Derry jazzman Gay

George (seated) and Neil Doherty.

McIntyre would always say "*Your father is the best jazz bass player in Ireland.*" That's how he made his living. He played in the resident band in the Embassy and was a top musician of his time. I have been told that Sally slaved at her sewing machine to send him to St. Columb's College.

My grandfather's murder has cast a long shadow over our lives. He had served throughout the First World War, was wounded three times, survived the war only then to be shot dead on the streets of Derry in a sectarian killing. What did this killing achieve? It left three children without a father. I feel angry about the futility of it. What did it achieve for the Loyalist cause at the time? Was it meant to intimidate others? Nobody was brought to justice though that wouldn't have brought him back.

My maternal grandmother's two brothers-in-law fought in the British Army during the First World War. One of them, Neil Doherty, served in France throughout the winter of 1914/1915 and was killed in action on May 16th, 1915. He is buried in Cabaret-Rouge Cemetery, Souchez, Pas de Calais, in France. He was the son of Mary Jane Doherty, 86 Lecky Road. His name is on the Diamond War Memorial. The other brother, George, was wounded. When he came back from the war, because of what he'd seen there, he said that there had to be a heaven and a hell - he had seen hell. George lived in Chamberlain Street.

George Doherty's grandson is the twice Turner Prize nominated artist Willie Doherty."

A postcard showing the Diamond Hotel (left corner). Edwin Andrew Price was shot dead at the door of the hotel.

Trevor Temple reflects upon

The riots of 1920

Tragically, Augustus Austin was not the only former First World War soldier to lose his life in the period of bitter sectarian blood-letting that engulfed the city of Derry/Londonderry during the months of May and June 1920.

Cruelly, several ex-military men who had survived the incessant barrage of shelling and machine-gun attack on the Western Front and elsewhere, were gunned down in the relative safety of 'Civvy Street.'

The first of these was Bernard Doherty, a Catholic, who was shot in Orchard Street on Sunday, May 16, 1920 and died within half an hour of receiving a gunshot wound to the chest. It appeared that Bernard, who was accompanied by a friend, went up to Orchard Street during a lull in riotous firing that same night. Suddenly shots rang out again and Bernard was struck in the chest. He turned and ran down the street, and, staggering along New Market Street, fell at Linenhall Street steps. People passing ran to his assistance and carried him down the steps to the house of a William Simms. A priest was sent for and quickly arrived and administered last rites.

Bernard Doherty had been gassed and wounded during the Great War. He was only twenty-one years of age. His brother, Private William John (Johnnie) Doherty, was killed five years earlier in action at the Dardanelles on May 23, 1915 (Whit Sunday), aged only 19. His remains are interred in Twelve Tree Copse Cemetery, Turkey, and his name is commemorated on the Diamond War Memorial.

One month later, during trouble in the Diamond area on the night of Saturday, June 19, 1920, a forty-five year old Protestant, Edwin Andrew Price, was shot. He had come to the door of the Diamond Hotel, where he was staying, when a bullet struck him in the abdomen. The ambulance at that time being engaged in another act of mercy, a number of Protestants got hold of a stretcher and carried the injured man to the Fire Station in Hawkin Street. He died shortly before midnight. Edwin Price was a brother of Albert Price, merchant, Shipquay Place. He had returned from the U.S.A. when the First World War broke out and served with the Ambulance Corps of the Ulster Division. He was about to return to America when he was fatally wounded.

Some years ago Buncrana resident, Paul Quigley, dug up a First World War shell case in his then garden at Castle Park in the town. It was engraved on one side and had the following inscription on the other:

Thiepval

16th 36th

Divisions

(Drawing of a harp shaking red hand)

World War Souvenir

From

EA Price

54652

BEF

(All of the above was enclosed within the shape of a heart)

A colleague of Paul's converted the shell into a small watering can. The inscription – carved by the same Edwin Price who lost his life at the Diamond in 1920 – obviously symbolised the coming together of the two traditions in Ireland on French soil. It is a bitter irony, then, that Edwin Price lost his life during fierce clashes involving those same traditions back home in Ireland.

On the morning of Monday, June 21, two days after the death of Edwin Price, James Dobbin, a Protestant worker, was attacked by a group of 'nationalists' at the bottom of Bridge Street, while on his way to work. He darted towards the quay but his attackers overtook him, knocked him down and kicked him. He tore himself away but the 'nationalists' shot him and he fell severely injured. As he was struggling to his feet, his pursuers lifted him up and threw him into the river. Two postal officials ran to Dobbin's aid but the 'nationalists' threatened to shoot them too and they were

The First World War shell converted into a watering can.
(Photograph courtesy of Jackie McColgan, Yes! Publications)

forced to abandon their attempted rescue. Dobbin remained struggling for a significant period in the water, hanging on to a boat, while the *'nationalists'*, at revolver point, kept at bay anyone who attempted to go to his assistance. Eventually, two policemen arrived and dragged Dobbin into a boat. He was transferred to the infirmary in a state of collapse. He died at two o'clock on the morning of Wednesday, June 30.

On the same day that James Dobbin received his fatal injuries, Howard McKay, aged about 25, the eldest son of Mr Marshall McKay, the then Governor of the Apprentice Boys of Derry, was murdered.

McKay, who served in the North Irish Horse in the First World War, had just arrived in the city from a holiday in Portstewart. He was on his way home, when a party of armed *'nationalists'* held him up, near the North-West Agricultural Show Grounds at Brandywell Road and shot him dead.

His body lay on the road for several hours, while his killers remained close at hand, preventing its removal. After some time a hearse coming towards the city was seized, the body was bundled into it and the driver commanded to turn back and take it to the house of Howard McKay's father at Braehead.

Dunree musicians to play tribute to World War I priest

A group of Inishowen musicians are to play a special part in ceremonies tomorrow marking the 90th anniversary of one of the most bitterly fought battles of WWI.

The Battle of Passchendaele became a symbol of the violence of war in its most gruesome and senseless form.

Now fiddlers Tracey and Donna McRory, both grandnieces of Dunree-born priest who was injured at Passchendaele, will honour him and his fallen comrades at the historic battlefield.

Fr. James McRory was one of three Derry priests who acted as chaplains during the First World War, along with Fr Hugh Smith of Moville and Fr.William Devine of Castlederg and Coleraine.

Fr McRory's diary, which opens with the poignant words 'In the Shamrock Dugout, at the trenches where Ypres once was', offers a moving firsthand account of this terrible time, which saw so many brave men endure unimaginable horrors.

He was with the 16th Irish Division at the Battle of Passchendaele when he was wounded on the 21st October 1917.

"I can't believe that ninety years on I have the honour of playing the violin in remembrance of, not only my granduncle, but also for all the young men from the Island of Ireland who died during that awful war' Tracey said this week.

"I have had the honour of Playing at the Menin Gate on the 11th November for the last couple of years. It's such an emotional experience. When I played 'Danny Boy' last year everyone started to sing and it was very, very moving."

Around 20,000 people are expected to attend this year's special anniversary.

Tracey, a four times All Ireland fiddle champion and noted harp player, worked with her partner Sam Starrett and local musician Richard Laird, writing new music and songs about the sacrifice of all the Irish soldiers. Their song 'John Condon' tells the story of a fourteen-year-old soldier killed in WWI. Three singers worldwide have recorded their own

Tracey McRory, Eilidh Patterson, Eddie O'Donnell and Donna McRory

❝ I can't believe that ninety years on I have the honour of playing the violin in remembrance of, not only my granduncle, but also for all the young men from the Island of Ireland who died during that awful war **❞**

McRory, Donna McRory and Eddie O' Donnell will perform four songs for this special concert.

Tracey added: "'It is so important to me that the songs Sam wrote will not be forgotten and, although this year he will not be with me in Ypres, his music will. Sam and I believed in the healing of music and when I stand and play at the Menin Gate this year on the 11th November I will be playing for Sam."

Very special

On the 20th November will perform one of Tracey's violin compositions, entitled 'Passchendaele' which she wrote for Sam's play 'Home for Christmas.

"It was only after I had written it that I found out my granduncle had been a Chaplin to the Irish forces during the

Musician and composer, Tracey McRory, playing at the Menin Gate.

Tracey McRory remembers
Fr. James McRory

" Father James McRory is my great-uncle. He was born in 1881 about a mile away from Dunree Fort in Inishowen. Growing up he went to the Desertegney National School and then later to St. Columb's College. He was a fine soccer player and he secured a special dispensation from St Columb's to play soccer for Derry Celtic.

He trained for the priesthood in Ireland. After his ordination in Rome (1909) he served in the Glasgow archdiocese of Croy in Lanarkshire between 1909 and 1914. At the outbreak of the First World War, he joined up as a chaplain, serving from 1914-1917. He was one of three local priests who acted as chaplains during the war, the others being Fr. William Devine of Castlederg and Fr. Hugh Smith from Moville. Like the Irishmen who answered John Redmond's call to fight for "the freedom of small nations", Fr. McRory had strong and often conflicting emotions.

Father James McRory, chaplain with the Connaught Rangers during the First World War.

His diaries often give us an insight into the reactions of a young priest confronted with totally unprecedented horror of the First World War, a monumental example of man's inhumanity to man.

I discovered all this seven years ago when I came across an article in Derrianna (a Derry Diocesan magazine) written by Father Desmond Mullan about my great-uncle in the First World War. This was the first time I had seen a picture of Father James, set a face to him or even knew he had served in the First World War. Father Mullan writes: *"When I was a young boy in my home in Coleraine, I remember seeing a photograph of Father McRory in his captain's uniform. A photograph of a young, handsome and happy man that was surely taken before this diary was written. So different is the picture which emerges from these pages."*

Reading Father Mullan's article set me off on a search to find and read the diaries myself. As a musician I had already composed a piece of music for "Home for Christmas". My partner Sam, who sadly died in 2007, had asked me to write a piece for the opening of this very special play. When I was searching for a name for the piece, I called it "Passchendaele"- simply because this is a beautiful, beautiful name even though a horrendous battle was fought there. A few years later, when I read my great-uncle's diary, I discovered that he was wounded on 21st October 1917 at the battle of Passchendaele! Somehow I was meant to write that piece about him.

Father James' diaries are an amazing human document. In one entry he talks about being in the trenches for six continuous weeks, six weeks spent under heavy shelling, not able to lift his head above the parapet. What kind of lasting effect would this have? I never met Father James but I fully believe that what he writes about was 'his truth' at the time. He was a very intelligent man and, in his diaries, he was very angry at what he witnessed. He was angry at top level inefficiency. He was very angry at the generals, at their ignorance of

From left to right, the late Sam Starrett, David Ferguson, Richard Laird and Tracey McRory, performing their piece, 'Harp and Crown' in front of President Mary McAleese, in Belgium.

what was happening and at the mistakes they made in different battles. He was really angry about how Irish soldiers had not been given the same respect, the same rewards and the same acknowledgements for bravery as had English soldiers. Being a Catholic priest, he was angry too at the shelling and destruction of convents and churches so they couldn't be used by snipers. He was angry that there was no respect for religion and what he held sacred. Throughout his diaries, he writes that the Germans knew that convents were a place of safety for mothers and children, who were being looked after by nuns, but yet they shelled them.

Sometimes I think of him as a young priest out there on the battlefields, hearing confessions, being the final port of call for young soldiers dying, hearing their last few words, maybe whispering an Act of Contrition in an ear, or taking letters and trying to deliver them to their mothers. When he came back, he very rarely talked about the war.

I struggled to find his diaries when I went to the Public Record Office in Belfast. His name is spelt 'McCrory' in the public records, but 'McGrory' in the Derrianna article. His actual name is James McRory. It took me two journeys to the Public Records Office to locate the diaries.

I recall that moment, sat at a table in the Public Record Office, opening the diaries, just me and his diaries. There was an instant connection. *"My God, did he leave these diaries in the hope that somebody would come along, not necessarily a member of the family but somebody and do something with them, tell his story. I have no doubt that the piece of music that I wrote, before I knew he existed or fought in the First World War, the music about Passchendaele is certainly about him and somehow looking at his diaries for the first time in his own handwriting has unleashed in me an energy to find out more. His diaries aren't for military historians, who want to know more about battlefield strategies and troops movements - even though that's in there - they are a human document and that's where they rank really high."*

There's other family who might know more about him. My dad and aunt both knew him after the Second World War, but not very well. There is a cousin in Buncrana, now in her 90's, who remembers him. After he was wounded at the Battle of Passchendaele, he was sent home. He came back to Scotland for a while and then he served as a priest in various parishes across Northern Ireland until his death in 1952, aged seventy-one, in Warrenpoint Nursing Home.

There are two shell casings that Father James brought back from the war that are still kept in our family home, in "the good room." These were given to him by a German officer and prisoner of war. The German officer had fashioned them both exactly the same. He had decorated them with pictures of a young girl with long hair. The shell numbers are on the bottom. They are made of brass and I used to think they were vases but never really thought to ask what they were. Nobody ever said what they were. When I was wee, if people were coming to visit, we had to polish them.

A few years ago I was asked by the Last Post Association to come and play at the famous Menin Gate for the Armistice Commemorations. In 2008, I was asked to write a special piece for the 90th Anniversary of the end of the war. I composed a piece called 'Bernard'. Bernard McGeehan, was executed by his own side in Poperinghe in November 1916. He was originally born in Raphoe but later moved to Moat Street in Derry with his family. In 2006 Bernard won a posthumous pardon.

Postscript

After going to Belgium in November 2008 and playing both at the Menin Gate and at Passchendaele, a woman contacted the family to tell us about a priest in a Florida nursing home, now in his nineties, who believes he has the chalice Father James used in the trenches. Father James had given the chalice to this priest when he was ordained, saying it was important and to look after it. The woman, a relative of the priest in Florida, wants the chalice to come back to Dunree, back to where Father James was born and is buried.

Somme back to the Foyle

Copyright: Songshed

Sam Starrett

Fifes and drums came up the street
the first day of July
its time for them to march again
but you let it pass you by
your medals polished on the shelf
and bowler in the hall
ah but after you came back from France
you never marched at all

CHORUS

At seventeen its hard to be upon a foreign soil
ah but its a long long way
from the Somme back to the Foyle
at seventeen its hard to bleed beneath a foreign sky
but seventeen's a ripe old age for boys like you to die

A mother's desperation and a heart so tired and sore
of faded yellow envelopes
and strangers at the door
as sons who witness summer turn
obscene and so absurd
ah but after you came back for France
you hardly spoke at all

CHORUS

What comfort to a women's heart
that one in five return
big hole in your shoulder and a heart so badly burned
you never spoke of what you saw
and you wouldn't march a step
ah but after you came back from France
you never did forget

CHORUS